MORE THAN
PETTICOATS

REMARKABLE
TENNESSEE WOMEN

Susan Sawyer

TWODOT

A · TWODOT · BOOK

1 2 3 4 5 6 7 8 9 10 BP 05 04 03 02 01 00

Design, typesetting, and other prepress work by Falcon® Publishing, Inc.

Cover photo: "Ten-minute break in the backyard, 1913." Courtesy of Girls Preparatory School, Chattanooga, Tennessee.

Project Editor: Charlene Patterson
Copyeditor: Kathryn McEnery
Page Compositor: Dana Kim-Wincapaw
Book design by Falcon® Publishing, Inc.

Library of Congress Cataloging-in-Publication Data

Sawyer, Susan.
   More than petticoats : remarkable Tennessee women/Susan Sawyer.
      p. cm.
   Includes bibliographical references and index.
   ISBN 1-56044-901-2
      1. Women—Tennessee—Biography. 2. Tennessee—Biography. I. Title.
CT3260.S29 2000
920.72'09768—dc21
   [B]
                                                          99-052359

Dedicated to the memory of three Tennessee women
whose ordinary lives seem remarkable to me:
my great-grandmother, Annie Mullins Adams (1879–1965),
and the grandmothers I never had the privilege of knowing,
Pearl Capitola Grimsley Spears (1885–1943)
and Irene Emma McDonald Adams (1900–1953).

Contents

6   Introduction

8   Nancy Ward
Beloved Woman

18   Rachel Donelson Jackson
Beloved Wife of "Old Hickory"

29   Sarah Childress Polk
First Lady

38   Eliza McCardle Johnson
First Lady

47   Elizabeth McGavock Harding
Mistress of Belle Meade Plantation

59   Elizabeth Meriwether Gilmer
Columnist Dorothy Dix

71   Ida B. Wells Barnett
Investigative Journalist and Social Reformer

81   Emma Bell Miles
Artist, Writer, and Poet

91 EMMA ROCHELLE WHEELER
Physician and Hospital Founder

97 SUE SHELTON WHITE
Suffragist and Political Activist

108 BESSIE SMITH
Empress of the Blues

118 GRACE MOORE
The Tennessee Nightingale

130 BIBLIOGRAPHY

135 INDEX

140 ABOUT THE AUTHOR

INTRODUCTION

Come along with me, and let's explore the lives of some remarkable women from Tennessee's past.

On the following pages, you'll find twelve women who made a difference in the world. All of the women were born before 1900. All have links to Tennessee. And each woman, in her own way, left her mark on history.

You'll probably recognize names like Rachel Jackson, wife of our seventh president, or Bessie Smith, the great blues singer. Others, like those of writers Emma Bell Miles and Ida B. Wells Barnett, may not be as familiar. But regardless of fame or obscurity, each deserves a place in history. Behind the names, the individual stories demonstrate determination to triumph over challenges, remarkable fortitude to overcome adversity, and courage to remain strong in difficult times.

As a native and resident of Tennessee, I share the common bond of statehood with these incredible women. While researching and writing their stories, I explored their lives on an intimate level. I walked along the same paths they once walked. I explored their homes, listened to their music, read their diaries, or lingered at their gravesites. And along the way, I developed a new appreciation for these women who once lived or worked in my home state.

I learned much more than I ever expected to learn. Before writing this book, I never truly comprehended the depths of the profound love between Rachel and Andrew Jackson. I never realized that Sue Shelton White, a Tennessee suffragist, faced imprisonment when she fought to gain access for women at the election polls. And

INTRODUCTION

I never knew that it was Elizabeth Meriwether Gilmer, a plain-spoken Tennessee woman, who gained fame and fortune as one of the most admired newspaper columnists in the world.

Now I'd like to share the stories of these remarkable women with you. You might laugh at some of their antics. You might cringe at some of the obstacles that they were forced to endure. But you will certainly gain a new appreciation for the Tennessee women who shaped and molded the course of our history.

Come along with me, and let's celebrate the lives of twelve remarkable women from Tennessee's past.

NANCY WARD

circa 1738–1822

Beloved Woman

$\mathcal{S}$urrounded by a thick haze of gun smoke and the thunder of rifles, Nanye´hi crouched behind the fallen log. She edged closer to her husband, Kingfisher, determined to help in their tribe's raging battle against the Creeks, the Cherokee's traditional enemy.

Another round of gunfire blasted through the woods, louder and more ominous than before. Realizing that the Creeks were getting closer, Nanye´hi reached for a pouch of bullets at her husband's side. Helping Kingfisher prepare his weapons was the least she could do.

Though still in her teens, Nanye´hi was well aware of the grave dangers of accompanying her warrior-husband into battle, and that the outcome of the Battle of Taliwa would determine the fate of their native Cherokee tribe.

She placed a bullet into her mouth, believing that chewing the lead bullet would make it much more deadly. She then handed the softened bullet to her husband as the gunfire continued around them.

Kingfisher had just placed another bullet into his rifle when a war-painted Creek abruptly leaped into sight. Nanye´hi gasped as the Creek aimed his rifle directly at her husband.

Kingfisher raised his rifle, but it was too late. The shot from the Creek's weapon was swift and deadly. Kingfisher let out a cry of pain just as a stream of blood spurted from his heart. He slumped lifelessly to the ground. The Creek disappeared into the woods, leaving Nanye'hi to mourn the sudden loss of her beloved husband. She cradled his listless body in her arms, tears springing to her eyes.

Like a clap of thunder, another blast of gunfire split through the air, jarring Nanye'hi back into reality. She brushed her lips against her husband's forehead, then quickly wiped her tears away. She would have the rest of her life to grieve over Kingfisher's passing. For the moment, she had to set aside her grief and continue the fight for her people.

She picked up Kingfisher's weapon just as two Cherokee braves darted up beside her. Letting out a blood-curdling war cry, she motioned for the braves to follow her into battle. Rallied by her bravery and determination, other tribesmen quickly fell into place behind the courageous young Cherokee woman. By the time the battle was over, Nanye'hi had led her people to a decisive victory over the Creeks.

News of Nanye'hi's valor at the 1755 Battle of Taliwa in present-day Canton, Georgia, quickly spread among the Cherokee tribe. Soon after Nanye'hi returned to her native home in the region now known as Tennessee, she was chosen to fill the vacant position of *Aqiqa-u-e*, or "Beloved Woman," of the Cherokees. Only women of great influence were awarded the title of Beloved Woman. It was the highest role that could be achieved by a female in the matriarchal Cherokee society. Also translated as "War Woman," the title was usually bestowed upon women warriors or the mothers or widows of warriors.

Although Nanye'hi had truly earned the honorable title by demonstrating her bravery in battle, it was unusual for the Cherokees to award the role to a female as young as she. When Nanye'hi received the title of Beloved Woman, she was only about eighteen years old. But throughout the remainder of her life, she would prove herself worthy of the honor, serving as an exceptional Cherokee leader for nearly fifty years under the name of "Nancy Ward."

Nanye'hi was born about 1738 at Chota, meaning "Peace Town" or "Mother Town," in the Overhill region of the Cherokee Nation. Her mother was called Tame Doe or Tame Deer, and her uncle was Attakullakulla, "Little Carpenter," civil chief of the Overhill Cherokees and an influential leader at the time of Nanye'hi's birth. Attakullakulla would later become the Wise Counselor of the Cherokee.

Most historians contend that her father was a Delaware, or Lenni Lenap, who joined the Wolf clan of the Cherokees by marriage to Tame Doe. Nanye'hi, a tribal name that translates to "Spirit People," was also related to such leaders as Old Hop, the emperor of the Cherokee Nation in the 1750s, and Osconostato, the Great Warrior of the Cherokee Nation.

Nanye'hi married the Cherokee warrior Kingfisher in her early teens and had already given birth to two children, Catharine and Fivekiller, by the time of the Battle of Taliwa. Many belive her legendary beauty earned her a Cherokee nickname meaning "Cherokee Rose" or "Wild Rose," since the Cherokee adored and cultivated wild roses throughout the region. Some insist the name compared the fine texture of her skin to the velvety smoothness of wild rose petals.

Her beauty and regal presence apparently impressed visitors to the Cherokee Nation as well. During a visit to the Cherokees in the early 1800s, the famous botanist Thomas Nuttall described Nanye'hi as "tall, erect, and beautiful, with a prominent nose, regular features, clear complexion, long, silken black hair, large, piercing, black eyes and an imperious air."

"Queenly and commanding" was James Robertson's impression of the Cherokee's Beloved Woman. Robertson, who served as North Carolina's agent to the Cherokee tribe, visited Nanye´hi at her home during the 1770s. He also reported that her residence was furnished in "barbaric splendor as befitted her rank in the nation."

But the rank of Beloved Woman was not merely an honorary position in the Cherokee Nation. Since the Cherokees believed the Great Being spoke through the Beloved Woman, a multitude of responsibilities accompanied the title. There was leadership of the Women's Council, comprised of representatives from each clan. There was also an influential voice and vote in the General Council of Chiefs. The Beloved Woman worked behind the scenes as well, as an ambassador or peace negotiator mediating between those who favored war and those who demanded peace.

One of the honors bestowed upon the Beloved Woman was the privilege of preparing the sacred "Black Drink"—tea used for ceremonial purification—and serving it to warriors before battle. She also had the right to save a condemned prisoner from execution.

In the late 1750s, Nanye´hi, Beloved Woman of the Cherokees, became known by yet another name, Nancy Ward. After the completion of Fort Loudon in 1757, several traders established quarters within the walls of the fort and took Indian wives. During this time, Nanye´hi—now called "Nancy" by the many non-Indians in the territory—became the wife of Bryant Ward, one of the Scot-Irish traders at the fort. Although the union produced a daughter, Elisabeth, the marriage ended sometime before 1760, when Ward returned to his white family and home in South Carolina.

Alone once again with three children to raise, Nancy must have known it would not be easy to fulfill her role as both mother and Beloved Woman. With the Royal Proclamation of 1763, the British empire recognized the rights of her people by denouncing further white settlement on Cherokee lands. But white settlers ignored the proclamation and continued to flood into the region, creating constant tension in Indian-white relations.

This intrusion by whites had been creating dissension among the Cherokees for years. During Nancy's childhood, her people had had mixed reactions to Moravian missionaries and their attempts to convert the Cherokees to Christianity. Resistant to change and intent on preserving their traditional customs and religion, some Cherokees regarded the missionaries as a threat. Others, eager to embrace the white man's ways, viewed their presence as a blessing.

Attakullakulla, Nancy's influential uncle, eventually allowed the Moravians into Cherokee territory, but only if they agreed to build schools for teaching the white man's ways and language to Cherokee youth.

Attakullakulla had grown up along the banks of the Little Tennessee and Hiwassee Rivers in eastern Tennessee. He promoted the interests of the Cherokee throughout his life, but his tactics often turned his own people against him. His bargain with the Moravians provoked some to claim he wanted the Cherokee people to accept the white man's ways; others viewed his plan as a way to teach the tribe more about the enemy.

Historians believe Attakullakulla's leadership and negotiation skills greatly influenced Nancy Ward in her role as Beloved Woman. Like her uncle, Nancy tried to find the middle ground between tradition and innovation as she assumed the leadership duties among her people.

As a member of the General Council of Chiefs, which decided whether or not to wage war, Nancy knew the details of approaching attacks by her people. But she staunchly disapproved of intentionally killing civilians, and her later deeds proved that she would not waver from her convictions. When militant Cherokees prepared to attack white communities near the Watauga River in July 1776,

Nancy warned settlers of the impending attack on Fort Watauga. With adequate time to fortify their forces, the settlers withstood a siege by the Cherokees for more than two weeks.

Not all of the fort's inhabitants escaped the Cherokee's wrath. Before she could reach the safety of the stockade, the Cherokees captured Lydia Bean, wife of William Bean, Tennessee's first permanent settler. The militant warriors condemmed her to death by fire and tied the woman to a stake at the top of a huge ceremonial mound. Upon learning of the woman's plight, Nancy immediately exercised her right as Beloved Woman to spare the condemned captive. When Nancy arrived at the scene, she reportedly declared, "No woman shall be burned at the stake while I am Beloved Woman!"

Obviously concerned about the woman's condition, Nancy took the injured captive into her own home at Chota to nurse her back to health. While under Nancy's care, the white woman taught the Cherokee leader how to set up a loom, spin thread or wool, and weave cloth. Nancy, in turn, passed these new skills on to her people.

The Cherokees must have welcomed the addition of comfortable, soft clothing to their meager wardrobes. Until Nancy introduced weaving to them, their attire consisted of traditional animal skin hides and rough, uncomfortable hemp articles purchased from traders. By learning the art of weaving, the Cherokees eventually became less dependent on traders.

But historians claim the skills also Europeanized the Cherokee in terms of gender roles. Women—traditionally the head of the household under the Cherokee's matriarchal society—soon were expected to do the weaving and household chores, while the male role in Cherokee society changed from warrior to farmer.

Lydia next brought her dairy cattle to Nancy's home, and the Cherokee woman learned the art of making butter and cheese from the milk of the white man's buffalo, which could provide some nourishment even when hunting was bad. Nancy, in turn, introduced dairy farming to the Cherokees. The tribe eventually amassed large herds, farms, and an abundance of slave labor for dairy farming. During the last half of the eighteenth century, many Cherokees became slave owners. In fact, Nancy became the first Cherokee slave owner in 1755 when her people rewarded her victory at the Battle of Taliwa with a Creek warrior as a slave.

When Attakullakulla died in 1778, Nancy became the chief arbitrator and peace keeper between the Cherokees and white settlers. She assumed the role during a critical period in Cherokee history: frontiersmen were waging battles against the British in the war for independence and struggles abounded between warring tribes. At the same time, a constant stream of white settlers poured into the Cherokee homelands, making the Cherokee war chief, Dragging Canoe, determined to drive whites from the country.

In 1780, British officers encouraged Dragging Canoe to attack the white settlements. Since many of the settlers had taken up arms against the British at the Battle of King's Mountain, the remaining whites in the settlements could not possibly defend themselves, the British reasoned.

Dragging Canoe agreed with the British advice. But as he prepared to assault the white settlements, Nancy once again warned the whites of an impending Cherokee attack. After receiving Nancy's warning, John Sevier, colonel of the Tennessee Militia, promptly organized a campaign against the Cherokees. Sevier and his men swept through the Cherokee Nation, burning many of the tribe's towns before Dragging Canoe had a chance to attack white communities.

By 1781, the white onslaught had crushed the Cherokees. But Nancy—who had learned the art of shrewd negotiation from her diplomat-uncle, Attakullakulla—knew how to use her diplomacy skills to serve the best interests of her people. Though she did not promote war, she refused to counsel for peace when she believed compromise would hurt her people. Her efforts as a negotiator earned her a prominent place in both American and Cherokee history.

During peace talks with Colonel Sevier at the Little Pigeon River in present-day Tennessee, Nancy became the first Indian female to actively engage in treaty negotiations. As the featured speaker for the Cherokee tribe, she pleaded, "Our cry is for peace . . . let your women's sons be ours; our sons be yours. Let your women hear our words." With her dramatic appeal for peace, Nancy essentially instructed Sevier to present the treaty to his "women" for ratification. Little did she realize that women at that time had no voice in matters of war and peace in the white man's world.

In the following years, the majority of Cherokees lived peacefully beside the whites, but there were episodes of violence and bloodshed as Dragging Canoe and his militant followers continued to attack white settlements. Nancy could not convince Dragging Canoe to halt the attacks, yet remained adamantly opposed to unnecessary violence. She demonstrated her convictions again by interceding on behalf of two white traders during a trade exchange in 1783.

The Cherokees found weapons hidden among the men's possessions, and they decided to kill them, believing the concealed weapons represented an act of aggression. But Nancy halted her people from killing the men, and the trade exchange continued without further incident.

Two years later, Nancy represented the Cherokee tribe as a peace negotiator at the signing of the Treaty of Hopewell, the first treaty between the Cherokees and the newly-formed United States. Nancy presented a symbol of friendship—a continuous strand of beads—to those gathered to negotiate peace. "We hope the chain of friendship will never more be broken," she said. It was her last public appeal for peace.

Nancy certainly realized that the Americans intended to acquire as much Cherokee land as possible and that her people might eventually be forced to leave their native soil. Fearing the American's quest for land would destroy her people, Nancy wisely counseled the tribe against land cession in 1808. As leader of the Women's Council, she issued a strong statement to the Cherokee people, urging them not to sell any more land to white settlers. By 1817, her desperation had become obvious. From her council seat, she informed the younger Cherokees to refuse any more requests for land—or take up arms against the Americans if necessary.

At the last council meeting in 1817, Nancy sent her walking cane to represent her. Some historians believe she resigned her position as Beloved Woman with this action, but most contend her physical absence was merely due to her advanced age and not an indication of resignation. Along with her walking cane, Nancy sent a written request to leaders, asking them to retain the remaining portion of Cherokee lands. Her wish was respected for only a few years. With the Hiwassee Purchase of 1819, all Cherokee lands north of the Hiwassee River—including Chota, Nancy's birthplace—were deeded to the Americans.

Throughout her remaining years, Nancy and her family operated an inn for travelers near her birthplace along the Ocoee River in eastern Tennessee. Although she must have been aware that the forced removal of her people to lands west of the Mississippi River was inevitable, she did not live to participate in the sorrowful experience of leaving her homeland. She died at her home about 1822, more than a decade before the Cherokees were forced to give up their native lands and be transported to Oklahoma territory along the "Trail of Tears."

Nancy's life passed into legend at her death. Under sworn testimony, her great-grandson reported that a light ascended from her body after her final breath, fluttered like a bird around the room, then left the house, moving in the direction of Chota. Some claim the light entered the most sacred mound in Chota, forever capturing Nancy's spirit.

Much more than a warrior, Nancy served as a superb spokesperson for her people and rendered wise counsel to her tribe. And her desire and efforts to exist peacefully with the whites personified the courage and spirit of the frontier people who sought peace and reconciliation during the turbulent settlement years between 1755 and 1820.

Today, Nancy Ward's burial site at Benton, Tennessee stands as a powerful symbol of courage, inspiration, and leadership among Cherokee women. Her grave marker, furnished by the Nancy Ward Chapter of the Daughters of the American Revolution (DAR), reads:

In Memory of Nancy Ward
Princess and Prophetess
of the Cherokee Nation
The Pocahontas of Tennessee
The Constant Friend
of the American Pioneer
Born 1738—Died 1822

Rachel Donelson Jackson

1767–1828

Beloved Wife of "Old Hickory"

Rachel Donelson Jackson stared at her husband in disbelief, stunned by the devastating news. How could anyone claim she was still married to her first husband?

She didn't understand; more than two years had passed since her first husband, Lewis Robards, had filed a petition with the Virginia legislature for a divorce. A few months after receiving word of the successful petition, Rachel had exchanged wedding vows with the love of her life, a young attorney by the name of Andrew Jackson.

Now, in 1793, Lewis was claiming that he'd never officially obtained the divorce. In reality, the Virginia legislature had merely granted him permission to file for a divorce in 1791—which he never bothered to do. Prompted by his own desire to remarry, Lewis had now filed for divorce from Rachel on grounds of adultery.

Infuriated by Lewis' charges, Andrew vowed that he and Rachel would remarry as soon as the legislature granted the divorce. And Andrew adamantly resolved that he would never allow anyone to mar his wife's "sacred name."

Rachel and Andrew Jackson quietly remarried in 1794. Since

Rachel Donelson Jackson

divorce was virtually unknown on the frontier during the late 1700s, the right to file a petition for a divorce could have been easily confused with the actual filing of a petition. But the mistake of marrying before Rachel's divorce was final would haunt the couple for the rest of their lives.

The future wife of the seventh president of the United States was born on June 15, 1767, in Accomac County, Virginia. As the tenth child of Rachel Stockley and Colonel John Donelson, Rachel was exposed to politics at an early age. Her father, the owner of a small iron foundry and vast land holdings in Pittsylvania County, was elected to the Virginia House of Burgesses in 1769. In 1779, Colonel Donelson organized a fleet of flatboats to carry household goods, livestock, and 120 women and children to a new colony on the Cumberland River in Tennessee. He also arranged to take his wife and their brood of eleven children—including twelve-year-old Rachel—to the frontier on his own flatboat, *The Adventure.*

Under the protection of forty frontiersmen, the flotilla journeyed down the Holston River to the Tennessee River, then floated from the Ohio to the Cumberland River. By the time the weary travelers arrived at Fort Nashborough in May 1780, they had floated nearly one thousand miles. Along the way, thirty-three people died from illness, drowning, or capture by Indians. The new settlement prospered in spite of smallpox and famines.

Wary of the Indians roaming the Cumberland Valley, however, Colonel Donelson temporarily moved his family to safer ground near Fort Harrodsburg, Kentucky. Living in Kentucky, Rachel blossomed into a beautiful young lady with a "beautifully moulded form" and "full red lips rippling with smiles and dimples." Her beauty captured the attention of handsome Lewis Robards, a member of a prominent local family. In 1785, at the age of eighteen, Rachel married Lewis in Mercer County and moved into his family's home in Harrodsburg.

But she immediately realized the marriage had been a dreadful mistake. Insanely jealous and hot-tempered, Lewis constantly accused Rachel of indiscreet behavior. And to make matters worse, Rachel's beloved family was no longer nearby for immediate help. Tragically, in 1785, the same year of Rachel's marriage, Colonel Donelson had been killed by Indians and her mother and siblings had returned to Tennessee.

By 1788, Rachel could no longer tolerate living with Lewis. Her brother, Samuel, traveled to Kentucky and returned with Rachel to their mother's home in Tennessee. She soon became acquainted with a tall, thin man by the name of Andrew Jackson. The young attorney was one of several boarders at the Donelson home, and had just assumed the position of public prosecutor in Fort Nashborough, now known as Nashville.

Meanwhile, Rachel's hot-headed husband sought out his wife in Nashville on several occasions. Rachel made several unsuccessful attempts at reconciliation with her husband and one historical account reveals that Rachel returned to Kentucky for a brief time to nurse Lewis' ailing mother. Each brief reunion, however, convinced Rachel that the marriage could not be saved.

The final breach occurred during early 1791 when Rachel heard rumors that Lewis was coming to Nashville with a posse of men to force her to return with him to Harrodsburg. Fearful for her life, she quickly arranged to visit relatives in Natchez, Mississippi. A family friend offered the use of a flatboat and organized a party of escorts for the river journey. Andrew Jackson, already known for his abilities as an Indian fighter, served as one of the escorts to assure Rachel's safety during the trip.

A few months later in Natchez, Rachel received word that Lewis had filed a petition for a divorce with the Virginia legislature. The legislature, she was told, had passed the bill. Now she was free to remarry.

Perhaps she was already contemplating remarriage by the time she received the news of her divorce from Lewis. Undoubtedly, she and Andrew had been attracted to each other for some time. As soon as Andrew heard of Rachel's divorce, the young attorney immediately asked for her hand in marriage. The couple became husband and wife in the fall of 1791.

After a marriage ceremony in Natchez and a honeymoon in Bayou Pierre, the newlyweds returned to Nashville. Rachel set up housekeeping while Andrew opened a law office on the public square and served as U.S. attorney for the state. Two years passed before they received the devastating news that Rachel's divorce had never been finalized. Hoping to forget the mistakes of the past and move forward with their lives, the Jacksons quietly remarried in 1794.

The validity of their first marriage ceremony remained an issue of contention. Unwilling to tolerate any attempt at marring Rachel's "sacred name," Andrew took grave offense at spiteful remarks about his wife's reputation. Heated conflicts and disputes often erupted between Andrew and those who dared to speak against Rachel's honor.

One such incident occurred in 1806 during an argument between Andrew and Charles Dickinson. The initial dispute concerned the forfeiture of a horse race, but the heated exchange soon led to unfavorable comments about Rachel and the Jackson marriage. Infuriated, Andrew promptly challenged Charles to a duel. Andrew mortally wounded the man, while a bullet from his opponent's dueling pistol remained lodged in Andrew's shoulder for the next twenty years.

Andrew's bold, aggressive personality had earned him the nickname of "Old Hickory" after military troops observed that he was tough as the wood of an old hickory tree. Yet in spite of his rugged—and sometimes rowdy—behavior, Rachel adored him. When his involvement in political and military affairs separated them for extended periods, she penned letters that conveyed the touching emotion of a woman who longed to be reunited with her husband. During one of Andrew's military expeditions, she wrote: "Shall I see you in twenty days? . . . Showers on scorching, withering grass will not be more reviving. . . . May the Lord . . . safely restore you to my arms in mutual love. . . ."

As time passed, Andrew and Rachel prospered. They acquired and sold tracts of land, bred and raced fine horses, and established stores in the new frontier. They settled into a large two-story home on their plantation, Hunter's Hill, and then later to the "Hermitage," a modest, three-room home located eight miles from Nashville. In 1819, Andrew completed construction of a new Hermitage, a two-story brick house with a double piazza. Today, this house stands as a lasting tribute to the rugged leader and his beloved wife and attracts thousands of visitors each year.

Although Rachel and Andrew never had children of their own, the doors of the Hermitage were always open to children. In 1809, the Jacksons became the adoptive parents of Andrew Jackson, Jr., one of Rachel's twin nephews. The child's mother, Lizabeth Donelson, had become sick after giving birth to the twins, and the Jacksons immediately rendered their assistance to the family. With five other children to care for, the Donelsons agreed to allow the Jacksons to adopt Andrew as their own. Another Donelson nephew came to live at the Hermitage after Rachel's brother, Samuel, was ambushed and killed in the early 1800s. Rachel and Andrew opened their hearts and their home to Andrew Jackson Donelson, one of Samuel's sons, and raised him as a member of their own family.

Apparently, children touched a soft spot in the heart of rugged Andrew Jackson. After defeating the Creek Nation in the historic Battle of Horseshoe Bend, the tough soldier could not ignore the distressed cries of a little boy who had been abandoned by his people during their defeat. Deciding to rescue the child, Andrew wrote a letter to Rachel in December 1813: "I have directed Major White to carry to you the little Lincoyer. . . . Charity and Christianity says he ought to be taken care of and I send him to my little Andrew and I hope you will adopt him as one of our family."

Andrew's constant involvement in political and military affairs frequently took him away from his family at the Hermitage. Elected to the House of Representatives in 1796, he briefly served in the U.S. Senate before accepting an appointment to the Tennessee Supreme Court in 1798. With his commission as Major General in command of the Army of Tennessee and service as the U.S. Secretary of War in 1812, Andrew rose to national fame. He became the hero and champion of the "common man" with his remarkable victory at the Battle of New Orleans on January 8, 1815.

Although Andrew's increasing popularity as a politician demanded many public appearances, Rachel avoided fanfare as much as possible. She preferred to remain at home; more than likely, she felt uncomfortable at sophisticated social gatherings. Raised as a child of the frontier, Rachel had received a sparse education and virtually no training in the rules of social etiquette. Even though guests at the Hermitage insisted she was a gracious, pleasant hostess, her simple, country ways did not impress the general public.

Yet, the appeal of celebrating Andrew's victory at the Battle of New Orleans was too difficult for Rachel to resist. Though she cared little for fashion or social events, she proudly accompanied her husband to a victory celebration. Observers, however, quickly noted that the "beautifully moulded form" of Rachel's youth had disappeared beneath a considerable amount of weight. One party guest described Rachel as a "short, fat dumpling bobbing" beside her tall, lanky husband on the dance floor.

Rachel's lack of sophistication and education became the target of snide remarks when she accompanied her husband to Washington in 1815. "Mrs. Jackson is . . . totally uninformed in mind and matters," one observer noted, "although extremely civil in her way."

Hardly oblivious to the insults, Rachel reluctantly accompanied Andrew to Florida during his brief term as governor of the territory in 1821. When Andrew was elected to the U.S. Senate in 1822, however, she opted to stay at home while Andrew worked on legislation in Washington, D.C.

But she ventured to the nation's capital during her husband's race for the presidency in late 1824. Though she rarely left her hotel room except to attend church services, Rachel agreed to attend a party in honor of her husband on January 8, 1825. Her presence at the event was far from a success. Guests claimed she was "stout, vulgar, [and] illiterate." One witness said attendees made "many repetitions of her ungrammatical speeches . . . the favorite form of spite." Andrew later confessed he had no idea his enemies would resort to such "wickedness" toward "a woman in her declining years."

Bitter and defeated, the Jacksons retreated to the Hermitage. Although Andrew won the popular vote during the 1824 presidential race, the House of Representatives voted to elect John Quincy Adams as president. Determined to win the next election, Andrew immediately began working on his next presidential campaign in 1828.

The heated race became one of the most vicious campaigns in the history of American politics. Although thirty-five years had passed since Rachel's divorce, Andrew's enemies constantly reminded the public of the controversy surrounding the Jackson marriage. Many argued that Rachel's background should prohibit her from assuming a prominent role in society. A North Carolina newspaper advised voters to consider "how they can justify it to themselves and posterity to place such a woman as Mrs. Jackson at the head of the female society of the U.S."

As rumors multiplied about Rachel's character, Andrew's campaign supporters sought evidence to prove that the Jacksons had not been truthfully informed about the status of Rachel's divorce at the time of their marriage. Still, the mud-slinging continued. One anti-Jackson campaign pamphlet stated: "Anyone approving of Andrew Jackson must therefore declare in favor of the philosophy that any man wanting anyone else's pretty wife has nothing to do but take his pistol in one hand and a horsewhip in another and possess her."

Though Rachel spent most of her time at the Hermitage during the heated presidential campaign, she made one public appearance with Andrew before the election. In January 1828, she traveled to Louisiana to celebrate the anniversary of the Battle of New Orleans. This time, instead of attacking her character, one observer took note of Rachel's plain appearance and her husband's obvious adoration by describing:

> A coarse-looking stout, little old woman, whom you might easily mistake for [Jackson's] washer-woman, were it not for the marked attention he pays her. . . . Her eyes are bright and express great kindness of heart; her face is rather broad, her features plain. . . . But, withal, her face is so good-natured and motherly, that you immediately feel at ease with her. Her figure is rather full, but loosely and carelessly dressed, so that when she is seated she seems to be settled into herself in a manner that is neither graceful nor elegant.

Despite the malicious campaign, Andrew won the presidential election by an overwhelming majority on November 24, 1828, defeating John Quincy Adams in his run for a second term of office. Rachel rejoiced for her husband's triumph, but her unpleasant experiences in the nation's capital remained vivid in her memory. When she received word of Andrew's victory, she said, "For Mr. Jackson's sake, I am glad," she said. "For my own part, I never wished for it."

Remaining at the Hermitage throughout the campaign may have shielded Rachel from many of the cruel attacks on her character. Soon after the election, however, a revealing conversation confirmed her worst fears. While shopping in Nashville, Rachel overhead a lively discussion about the recent election—and discovered that the scandal surrounding her divorce had become one of the major topics of the campaign. To her dismay, she realized her "sacred name" had been mocked and scandalized, handicapping the success of her beloved Andrew. By the time she returned to the Hermitage, the house servants reported that their mistress looked as though she had been "shot through the heart."

Distressed by such unsettling news, Rachel suffered a heart attack. Andrew constantly remained by her bedside until her death on December 22, 1828. Deeply resentful of the attacks on his beloved wife, Andrew said, "I can forgive all who have wronged me, but I will have to pray fervently that I may have the grace to enable me to forget or forgive any enemy who has ever maligned that blessed one who is now safe from all suffering and sorrow, whom they tried to shame for my sake."

Rachel Donelson Jackson was buried in her garden at the Hermitage on Christmas Eve, 1828, wearing the white dress she had purchased for her husband's inaugural ceremonies. The epitaph on her grave marker, penned by Andrew, reflects both his love for his wife and his bitterness at the campaign slurs that provoked her death:

> Here lies the remains of Mrs. Rachel Jackson, wife of President Jackson, who died the 22nd of December 1828, aged 61. Her face was fair, her person pleasing, her temper amiable, her heart kind; she delighted in relieving the wants of her fellow creatures, and cultivated that divine pleasure by the most liberal and unpretending methods;

to the poor she was a benefactor; to the rich an example; to the wretched a comforter; to the prosperous an ornament; her piety went hand in hand with her benevolence, and she thanked her Creator for being permitted to do good. A being so gentle and so virtuous, slander might wound but could not dishonor. Even death, when he tore her from the arms of her husband, could but transport her to the bosom of God.

SARAH CHILDRESS POLK

1803–1891

First Lady

*W*hile attending a small social gathering of politicians and their wives in the nation's capital, Sarah Childress Polk listened intently as her husband discussed the issue of federal banking with his fellow congressmen. Keenly interested in political topics, Sarah was well aware that her spouse, Tennessee Congressman James Knox Polk, supported President Andrew Jackson's position on the use of gold and silver as exchange mediums.

But experience had taught Sarah that paper money would be a far more practical choice for the American public. During a recent journey from Tennessee to Washington, D.C., she had pointed out to James that gold and silver coins were difficult to transport—and much too heavy for women to carry.

Now, listening to the conversation, Sarah couldn't resist the opportunity to share her travel experiences with the group. She quickly described the difficulties of her efforts to retrieve several small money bags from a trunk so she and James would have enough money in hand to pay their traveling expenses for the day. Finishing the story, she concluded that ladies could scarcely carry enough money with them because of the heavy weight of gold and silver coins.

Sarah Childress Polk

Several congressmen applauded Sarah's frank assessment of the inconvenience of using gold and silver as a circulating medium during the early 1830s. Sarah Childress Polk always voiced her opinion, even if her viewpoint was not the most popular choice. In an era when a woman's primary role in life consisted of marriage and motherhood, Sarah stepped beyond acceptable boundaries and took an active role in her husband's career. Well-educated and highly intelligent, the wife of the nation's second president from Tennessee adhered to a strong sense of values that greatly influenced the American public during the nineteenth century.

Born in 1803, Sarah was the third child of Elizabeth Whitsett and Joel Childress, a wealthy merchant and farmer. The Childress family consisted of six children—Sarah, Anderson, Susan, Benjamin, John, and Elizabeth—although Benjamin and Elizabeth died during early childhood. In 1808, Joel relocated his family from Sumner County, Tennessee, to a large plantation in Rutherford County near Murfreesboro. Five years later, Joel became Murfreesboro's first postmaster, holding the position for the remainder of his life.

Sarah grew up on the plantation in Rutherford County, receiving a basic education through private tutoring sessions with the principal and founder of Bradley Academy in Murfreesboro. The wealth of the Childress family permitted her to expand her knowledge as a pupil at the Moravian Academy in Salem, North Carolina—one of the few educational institutions open to female students in the early nineteenth century. Although Joel's death in August 1819 prompted Sarah to leave school and return to Murfreesboro, her studies at the academy provided her with a strong educational background.

Shortly after returning home from school, Sarah renewed her acquaintance with an ambitious young man by the name of James Knox Polk while attending a reception hosted by the governor. Years earlier, Sarah had met James when he was a student in Murfreesboro. A North Carolina native, James had moved to Tennessee with his family at age eleven. To further his education, he had returned to his native state for additional studies and graduated from the University of North Carolina with high honors in 1818. Two years later, he established a law practice in Columbia, Tennessee.

Soon after renewing his friendship with Sarah, James was elected to the Tennessee legislature as a Maury County representative. The legislative position demanded his frequent presence in Sarah's hometown of Murfreesboro, the state capital during the early 1800s. James seized these opportunities to become better acquainted with the dark-haired beauty. Legend contends that Andrew Jackson encouraged the romance between the couple.

On New Year's Day 1824, James Polk and Sarah Childress were married in a Presbyterian ceremony. The bride was twenty years old; the groom was twenty-eight. James's father, Samuel Polk, presented the couple with a two-story house in Columbia as a wedding gift.

James proved to be a popular Tennessee politician and won a seat in the U.S. House of Representatives in 1825. The long journey between Tennessee and the nation's capital was difficult, and the couple decided that Sarah would remain at home during James's first term as a congressman. James did not enjoy the separation from his wife, expressing his displeasure with the situation in a letter to Sarah: "It is terribly lonely here without you, still I'm glad I did not subject you to the hardships of the trip. However, this will be the last time I will be a Washington bachelor. Next year, I will bring you with me, for I am going to make reservations for decent accommodations for us before this session is over."

True to his word, James returned to Washington in 1826 with his wife at his side. The couple lived at a boarding house on Pennsylvania Avenue with other congressional families.

Between 1825 and 1839, James served seven consecutive terms in Congress. During those fourteen years, the Polks spent their winters in Washington and summers in Tennessee. Sarah displayed great interest in her husband's career, often sitting in the gallery of the House of Representatives as James debated issues of concern with fellow congressmen.

During Andrew Jackson's presidency, the Polks were frequent guests at the White House. Considered President Jackson's political protégé, James staunchly supported the political policies of his fellow Tennessean. He also served as Speaker of the House during Jackson's second presidential term.

Although Sarah was her husband's strongest supporter, she constantly worried about James's health throughout his political career. During lengthy campaign trips, she expressed concern in her letters to him by writing:

> When I think of the labor and fatigue you have to undergo, I feel sad and melancholy, and conclude that success is not worth the labor. . . . I . . . think that I can be as happy with my husband at home [as a] defeated candidate, as to have a successful one always from me. . . . All my fears are you cannot stand the hard labour of the canvass. I am not patriotic enough to make sacrifices for my country. I love myself (I mean my husband) better or more than my country. . . . We beg and pray that you will take care of yourself. . . .

In spite of Sarah's warnings, the pressures of political life took a toll on James, causing him weight loss, fatigue, and insomnia. So after serving four years as House Speaker, James retired from Congress in 1839 and returned to Tennessee to resume his private law practice. However, he could not resist the idea of returning to the local political scene. At the end of a heated campaign that took him all over Tennessee on horseback, the former congressman won the 1839 election for Tennessee governor.

When his race for a second term as governor resulted in defeat in 1841, James resumed his private law practice once again. But he returned to the political spotlight when Andrew Jackson pushed for James as a presidential candidate at the 1844 Democratic convention. Delegates selected James on the ninth ballot, making him the first "dark horse" candidate (a person unexpectedly chosen by a major party as a candidate for public office) in American politics. With the strong support of Andrew Jackson, who was known as "Old Hickory," James's supporters were soon referring to him as "Young Hickory."

After James defeated Henry Clay, the Whig Party candidate, in the 1844 presidential election, the Polks prepared to return to Washington. Sarah assumed her new role of First Lady with grace and ease, backed by fourteen years of experience as the wife of a prominent congressman. To the surprise of many, the Polks moved into the White House without making any changes to the private living areas that had been previously occupied by John and Julia Tyler. According to a New York newspaper:

> A couple of upholsterers who went from this city to procure so much of the job as falls within their department, came back with very reduced expectations. They were referred to the President's Lady, who gave them a courteous interview of 3/4 of an hour, but told them that only the public rooms would require repairs, for if the private apartments had been satisfactory to Mrs. Tyler, they would be so to herself.

With no children of her own, Sarah devoted herself to the needs of her husband and the daily management of the White House. Well aware of his wife's astute knowledge of politics, James trusted Sarah's keen insight and judgement. He frequently consulted her on political issues and asked for her assistance in writing his speeches.

To keep abreast of current events, she constantly read newspapers and magazines, giving her husband important articles that she thought he should read.

A skilled conversationalist who often predicted the sway of political trends with astonishing accuracy, Sarah knew the value of establishing and maintaining social contacts that would benefit her husband. Still, she restricted the number of social events at the White House, fearful that excessive social activities could sap James's physical energy. Throughout their residency in the executive mansion, the Polks welcomed guests only on Tuesday and Friday evenings.

Family members were exempt from Sarah's restriction on visitors. Relatives of both James and Sarah frequently visited the White House, and several kinfolk stayed for lengthy periods. Sarah's niece, Johanna Rucker of Murfreesboro, arrived for a visit in October 1845 and remained for nearly two years. And James Knox Walker, one of James's nephews who served as his private secretary, actually lived at the White House throughout the Polk presidency, along with his wife and children.

Although aware of the importance of maintaining political and social contacts, Sarah Polk refused to compromise her personal convictions for the sake of acceptance by others. A devout Presbyterian, she opposed drinking, dancing, attending horse races, and visiting the theater. Her personal beliefs became White House policies during her husband's term of office.

Although most historical accounts claim that the Polks never served liquor at the White House, the diary of one congressman's wife revealed that wine was served at one White House dinner in December 1845. One of forty guests at the four-hour event, the woman claimed that glasses with six different wines, ranging from pink champagne to ruby port, "formed a rainbow around each plate."

When Sarah prohibited dancing at the White House, critics insisted she was being too strict and pompous. In response, she replied, "Would you dance in so public a place as this? I would not. To dance in these rooms would be undignified and it would be respectful neither to the house nor to the office."

Others applauded Sarah's actions. The *Nashville Union* praised her decision to prohibit dancing by writing:

> The example of Mrs. Polk can hardly fail of exerting a salutatory influence. Especially does it rebuke the conduct of those ladies who professing godliness nevertheless dishonor its profession by their eager participation in the follies and amusement of the world. However, politicians may differ in regard to the merit of Mr. Polk's administration, there can be no difference as respects that of his lady, in her department of the Presidential mansion.

Sarah weathered personal attacks with aplomb, never wavering from her strong beliefs. In consideration of her husband's political standing, however, she attempted to convey her opinions with tact and grace to avoid offending others. But her tactful manner disappeared when anyone dared to criticize her husband. An entry in James's diary revealed: "Upon two or three occasions, I had decided that John Van Buren should be invited to dinner, and in each case Mrs. Polk has countermanded the order. . . . Amused when she told me she burned John Van Buren's dinner ticket. During the past year, he has been traversing the country making violent political speeches against my administration."

At the end of James's term of office, the Polks returned to Tennessee and moved into their new home in Nashville, "Polk Place." But James did not live to enjoy retirement at his new residence. Three months after leaving the White House, James K. Polk died on June 15, 1849.

Widowed at age forty-five, Sarah resided at Polk Place for the remainder of her life. Though James was initially buried in the city cemetery, his remains were transferred to Polk Place after Sarah supervised the construction of a monument in his honor on the grounds of the property.

Always clad in black mourning attire, Sarah rarely ventured from her home after the death of her husband. But she graciously welcomed many distinguished guests at Polk Place, including President Rutherford B. Hayes and his wife, Lucy. During the Civil War, both Union and Confederate officers regarded Polk Place as neutral ground, often stopping to pay their respects to the former First Lady. Communication with the outside world became reality for Sarah when the first Nashville telephone was installed at Polk Place on September 1, 1877.

In later years, Sarah enjoyed the company of her niece, Sarah Polk "Sallie" Jetton. Sallie moved into her aunt's home after the death of her mother. She continued to reside at Polk Place after her marriage to George William Fall and the birth of their daughter, Saidee Polk Fall.

Sarah maintained a sharp memory during her last years of life, granting newspaper interviews and vividly recalling details of political campaigns. She officially opened the Cincinnati Centennial Exposition, a commemoration of Ohio's progress over the last century, on July 4, 1888. The installation of telegraph wires at Polk Place allowed Sarah to touch an electric button and start the machinery that opened the exposition.

Sarah Childress Polk survived her husband by more than forty years, dying peacefully at her home on August 14, 1891, at the age of eighty-eight. After her death, the grave of James Polk was transferred to the grounds of the state capitol. Sarah was buried in a double tomb beside her husband, a befitting place of honor for the First Lady who devoted her life to the eleventh president of the United States.

ELIZA MCCARDLE JOHNSON

1810–1876

First Lady

*T*he chimes of a clock rang through the second floor of the White House, signaling the end of another long afternoon for Eliza McCardle Johnson. Earlier in 1868, the House of Representatives had charged her husband, President Andrew Johnson, with high crimes and misdemeanors in his handling of a defeated Confederacy. For the last three months, the United States Senate had been debating Andrew's fate. Now, Eliza was waiting to hear the outcome of the Senate's impeachment trial.

Throughout the long ordeal, Eliza had secluded herself in the family's living quarters on the second floor of the White House. Each evening, she received reports about the day's events from a steward who had been designated to attend the daily Senate proceedings. Though Eliza knew Andrew was facing the political battle of his life, she adamantly predicted he would not be convicted. Still, she was anxious for the trial to come to an end.

Soon, the steward arrived with his daily report, and Eliza learned that the trial was finally over. To convict the president of a crime, approval was need by two-thirds of the Senate. The final ballot was thirty-five to nineteen. President Andrew Johnson had been acquitted

Eliza McCardle Johnson

by a single vote. Just as Eliza had predicted, the Senate trial had vindicated the president.

During the difficult days of Andrew's impeachment trial in 1868, Eliza supported her husband with unwavering faith. Not much is known, however, about the private life of Eliza Johnson. Poor health forced her into seclusion for most of her adult life. But although she quietly remained in the background during nearly fifty years of marriage to Andrew, she offered constant encouragement and support to her husband in the midst of his political conflicts.

Personal acquaintances insisted that Eliza and Andrew Johnson were devoted to each other. A White House guard described the couple as "two souls and minds merged into one," while one Tennessee politician observed: "Their temperaments were unlike—he, fervid and aggressive; she, calm and retiring—but their union was fortunate, and by her aid, he was better prepared for the long encounter which fate held in reserve."

Born on October 4, 1810, Eliza was the daughter of Sarah Phillips and John McCardle, a shoemaker from Scotland. John briefly operated an inn in Greene County, Tennessee before establishing himself as a shoemaker in Greeneville, the county seat. By the early 1830s, the small village boasted of a population of nearly five hundred citizens, a local academy for young students, and its own academic institution, Greeneville College. Two other colleges in the immediate vicinity, Washington and Tusculum, also offered residents opportunities to further their education.

During her childhood in Greeneville, Eliza received a basic education at the local school, Rhea Academy. Local legend claims she and her girlfriends noticed Andrew Johnson on the September day in 1826 that he arrived in Greeneville, driving a small cart pulled by a blind pony. "There goes my beau, girls, mark it!" Eliza reportedly said to her friends.

Little did she realize that the handsome, dark-haired man who snared her attention was looking for a place to open a tailor shop. The son of a porter and a maid who worked at a North Carolina inn, Andrew had left his apprenticeship with a local tailor before fulfilling his service obligations. When his master offered a ten-dollar reward for his safe return, Andrew fled to Tennessee.

As he searched for a place to establish his business, Andrew must have been enchanted with the scenic view of the Great Smoky Mountains from the village of Greeneville, one of the oldest towns in Tennessee. And he must have been equally enamored by Eliza McCardle as he got to know her. Although he moved briefly to nearby Rutledge, Andrew could not forget the attractive, blue-eyed brunette from Greeneville. By the spring of 1827, he had returned to the village and proposed to Eliza.

Eliza McCardle became the wife of Andrew Johnson on May 17, 1827, in Warrensburg, Tennessee, a small town in Greene County. The justice of the peace who performed the wedding ceremony was Mordecai Lincoln, a second cousin of Abraham Lincoln. At the time of the marriage, Eliza was barely sixteen years old; the groom was eighteen. History shows that the Johnsons were the youngest to marry of all presidential couples.

Andrew rented a house on Main Street in Greeneville for his young bride. They established their living quarters in the rear of the building and converted the front portion into a tailor shop. Andrew could spell and read, but Eliza taught him the basics of writing and arithmetic. As he worked at his trade, he listened as Eliza read aloud to him. Drawn to politics, he practiced speeches while Eliza listened and offered suggestions. Soon Andrew discovered he enjoyed public speaking and joined a debating society at Greeneville College.

In 1828, Andrew won his first bid for public office when his fellow citizens elected him to serve as a Greeneville alderman. Though their first child, Martha, was born the same year, Eliza continued to tutor her husband. After Martha's birth, four more children arrived in the Johnson household: Charles in 1830; Mary in 1832; Robert in 1834; and Andrew, Jr., known as Frank, in 1852.

With Eliza's assistance, Andrew continued to improve his public speaking abilities and progressed in his political career, winning the position of mayor of Greeneville. Later, Andrew served six years in the Tennessee legislature. All the while, Eliza stayed at home, tending to the children and managing several properties and buildings that she and Andrew had purchased in the area.

In 1843, Andrew left for Washington, D.C. for his first term as a U.S. congressman from Tennessee. Eliza remained at home in Greeneville, following the tradition of many congressmen's wives who did not choose to venture to the nation's capitol with their husbands. While living alone in Washington, however, Andrew frequently enjoyed the company of his eldest child, Martha, a student at the local Georgetown Female Seminary.

A decade later Andrew was elected governor of Tennessee, taking the oath of office on October 17, 1853. Undoubtedly, Andrew's own lack of formal schooling influenced his strong support of public education. Public schools in Tennessee received funding for the first time during Andrew's first term as governor.

During the same period, Andrew and Eliza moved into a larger home in Greeneville, and both of their daughters became engaged. Mary became the wife of Daniel Stover, a Carter County farmer, in 1852, while Martha married Judge David T. Patterson in 1855.

Andrew's political career continued to advance with his election to the U.S. Senate in 1857. Once again, however, Eliza chose to stay at home in Greeneville while Andrew worked in Washington and lived alone in a small hotel.

The arrival of the Civil War brought changes to the lives of the Johnson family. In 1862, President Abraham Lincoln sent Andrew to Nashville to serve as the state's military governor. Staunch supporters of the Confederacy despised Johnson, a Southerner, for his allegiance to the Union.

In the summer of 1862, Confederates seized the Johnson's Greeneville home for use as a military hospital. Expelled from her residence, Eliza moved to the home of her daughter and son-in-law, Mary and Daniel Stover, in Carter County, Tennessee. By October, however, the Rebels forced Eliza to leave again. Accompanied by the Stovers and two of her sons, Charles and Frank, Eliza fled Carter County. The group arrived in Murfreesboro on a rainy evening and spent the night on the floor of an unheated house.

At six o'clock the next morning, Eliza and the rest of the family were summoned to appear before Confederate General Nathan Bedford Forrest. Since the area was under Confederate occupation, the general instructed Eliza to board the next train and return home, declaring that no one would be allowed to cross Confederate lines— not even Jesus Christ himself. Fortunately, the intervention of an influential state politician allowed Eliza and her family to proceed the next day and join Andrew in Nashville.

The tumultuous journey was exhausting for frail Eliza. In December 1862, the Stovers took her to Vevay, Indiana, a small town overlooking the Ohio River, seeking a cure for her suspected tuberculosis. Andrew's letters from Nashville expressed concern for his wife, sending "the best wishes of a devoted husband's heart."

Eliza's health continued to deteriorate after the deaths of two family members. Her son Charles, an army surgeon, died in April 1863 as the result of a tragic fall from a horse. The following year, Mary's husband, Daniel Stover, a Union soldier, died of consumption.

Although Eliza must have been extremely proud of her husband when he was inaugurated as vice president of the United States on March 4, 1865, her poor health prevented her from attending the ceremony. When Andrew assumed the presidency the next month after the assassination of President Lincoln, Eliza and the rest of the family prepared to move to Washington.

In June 1864, Eliza arrived in the nation's capitol to live at the White House. She settled into a second-floor room that became the center of activities for the large Johnson household. Family members living in the White House included two sons; the Johnson's widowed daughter, Mary Stover, and her children; and their daughter and son-in-law, Martha and David T. Patterson, and their children. Evidently, Eliza's grandchildren enjoyed her company. Historical accounts reveal that the children scurried to Eliza's rooms as soon as they finished their lessons each day.

With Eliza's frail health, daughter Martha assumed the role of hostess at White House functions. Upon their arrival in Washington, Martha immediately announced, "We are plain folks from Tennessee, called here by a national calamity. I hope not too much will be expected of us." To support her claim, Martha planted two cows on the lawn to supply fresh milk and butter and covered the mansion's threadbare carpets with simple muslin.

On New Year's Day 1866, Martha hosted the Johnson administration's first White House reception. With Eliza confined to her private quarters, Martha garnered the reputation of a gracious, competent hostess, even maintaining a regular social calendar during her father's 1868 impeachment trial.

Though fragile, Eliza remained the central core of the family's life in the White House. An avid reader, she saved newspaper and magazine articles that she thought would be of interest to her husband, presenting him with "good" news at the end of each day while saving the "bad" news for the next morning. One historical account contends that Andrew "may have consulted his wife and daughters more than he did any fellow statesmen."

During Andrew's term at the White House, Eliza made only two public appearances. Though she appeared briefly during a dinner in honor of a royal visit by the queen of Hawaii, a coughing spell prompted her to politely excuse herself from the festivities. She also attended Andrew's sixtieth birthday party at the White House, greeting guests upon their arrival. Party guests included several hundred children who had been invited to meet the president's five grandchildren, who ranged in age from eight to thirteen.

Andrew failed to win his bid to be the Democratic candidate for the 1868 presidential election, and the Johnsons returned to Tennessee. Son Robert committed suicide in 1869, unable to overcome a battle with alcoholism. The couple's sole surviving son, Frank, consoled his parents by promising never to indulge in any form of intoxicating liquors.

Back in Greeneville, Andrew grew restless in retirement, while Eliza's health continued to decline. In June 1871, Andrew wrote to his daughter, Martha:

> Your mother does not seem very well today, continues in bed, yet complaining of nothing unusual, with less cough than common. Mary is away and none of the family have been over to see her today. . . . If convenient it would be well enough to come down tomorrow, and perhaps it would have some influence on her mind and spirits. The House seems abandoned by all and I am so solitary as though I were in the wilds of Africa.

In spite of his political defeats on a national level, Andrew attempted to resume his political career by again running for the U.S. Senate. In 1874, he became the first former president to be elected to the Senate—the same body that had once tried to convict him. After hearing the news, Martha wrote to her father, "Your cup of joy is already full, and ours too great to express. . . . I feel it is the greatest victory of your life."

Once again, Andrew left for Washington, D.C., re-entering the Senate in 1875 to represent Tennessee. But the senator did not live to fulfill his term of office. After returning home for a relaxing visit with Eliza and his family, Andrew Johnson died on July 31, 1875. Eliza survived her husband by six months, dying at the home of her daughter, Martha Patterson, in 1876.

Today, visitors to the Andrew Johnson Historic Site in Greeneville, Tennessee can tour the tailor shop and modest residence where Andrew and Eliza lived as teen newlyweds, as well as the family's 1851 homestead with original furnishings. Located a short distance away is the Andrew Johnson National Cemetery, which contains the gravesites of Eliza, Andrew, and other family members. The Andrew Johnson Museum-Library on the campus of Tusculum College contains over five thousand Johnson artifacts, ranging from Andrew's law books to Eliza's dainty slippers. Andrew served as a member of Tusculum's board of trustees for thirty-five years.

Although Greeneville's historic sites are befitting memorials to Eliza and Andrew Johnson, most of Eliza's life remains clouded in mystery because of her lack of visibility during Andrew's career. In the absence of papers and correspondence, prospective biographers have obtained little information about the elusive First Lady. Only two copies of her signature are known to exist. Still, Eliza McCardle Johnson was a powerful influence on the nation's seventeenth president. Along with teaching her husband basic skills that would advance his career, she demonstrated unwavering faith and support throughout the difficult days of his presidency. And in spite of a life of confinement and ill health, Eliza deserves much of the credit for Andrew Johnson's ascent to the White House from his modest tailor shop in Greeneville, Tennessee.

ELIZABETH McGAVOCK HARDING

1819–1867

Mistress of Belle Meade Plantation

*T*he thunder of galloping horses shattered the pre-dawn silence of a spring Sunday in 1863 as a band of Confederate soldiers plundered across the magnificent Belle Meade plantation near Nashville. Laughing and cursing, the soldiers halted in front of the manor house and dismounted.

Awakened by the commotion, Elizabeth McGavock Harding ran to the window and gazed across the front lawn. About a dozen Confederates were milling over the grounds, obviously drunk and looking for trouble. Several men were hurling a rope over the limb of a large tree, while others were staggering toward the main entrance of the mansion.

At that instant, soldiers banged on the front door. In slurred voices, they demanded to see two Federal soldiers who had been assigned to guard the plantation. Elizabeth cringed, wishing she could turn to her husband for help. Since General William Giles Harding was not home at the moment, Elizabeth knew she had to take swift action. She hastily threw a cloak over her nightgown, grabbed a loaded pistol, and flew down the stairs.

Elizabeth McGavock Harding

Elizabeth hurled open the front door and stepped onto the porch. Aiming the pistol directly at the leader of the group, she demanded that he and his troops leave the premises at once. As the lone woman faced the party of drunken soldiers, the leader edged back in stunned disbelief. He quietly removed his hat and gallantly bowed to the mistress of Belle Meade. Then, pivoting on his heel, he turned to address his men. "Mount and get away, boys!" he called. "We don't want to disturb no lady as game as that!"

The soldiers hastily retreated from the plantation. Servants rushed to the front entrance and clamored around Elizabeth, joined by the two Federal guards whose lives had been spared from the Confederates' lynching rope due to her courageous defense. As the Federal soldiers expressed their thanks for her brave actions, Elizabeth modestly brushed aside their praise, saying:

> But what else could I have done? General Harding being away, our fighting force was not strong enough for that number, even if we shot from the window. I was therefore certain that if I went to the door, pistol in hand, they would at least pause: and then seeing one lone woman, they would be ashamed to do violence, for even the roughest men of our country have some good in them; and you see I was right.

The bravery of Elizabeth McGavock Harding garnered admiration from John "Jack" Ellerson Brown, one of the two Federal soldiers assigned to guard Belle Meade. Observing her courageous defense of home and family on that fateful Sunday morning, he suddenly realized "from what source the Confederate solider drew a double inspiration for his valor, backed as he was by the brave and self-sacrificing women of the South."

But defending Belle Meade from Confederate intruders was

not the only brave feat of Elizabeth McGavock Harding. When her husband was arrested and imprisoned during the Civil War, Elizabeth worked tirelessly to care for her loved ones while assuming her husband's responsibilities at the plantation. Primarily through Elizabeth's heroic efforts, Belle Meade survived the Civil War to become the "Queen of Tennessee Plantations," gaining fame and praise for its fine thoroughbred horses and gracious hospitality. Placing honor above all else, Elizabeth served as inspiration to others who encountered heartaches and losses throughout the War Between the States.

The daughter of Randal and Sarah Rodgers McGavock, Elizabeth Irwin McGavock was born on May 17, 1819. Randal McGavock, a prominent citizen who held several political offices in the area, was elected mayor of Nashville in 1824. Two years later, he completed the construction of an illustrious home for his family near Nashville. Named in honor of the McGavock's ancestral home in County Atrium, Ireland, the house was known as Carnton.

Raised at Carnton, Elizabeth became a poised young woman with a lovely singing voice who often played the piano and entertained guests with her musical talents. With the family's political and social connections, Carnton was the scene of many social events that included guests such as Andrew Jackson, Sam Houston, and James Polk.

By the late 1830s, Elizabeth's poise and beauty had attracted the attention of William Giles Harding, a member of another prominent local family. A graduate of the American Literary, Scientific and Military Academy in Middletown, Connecticut, William became known as "General Harding" after he was elected brigadier general of the Sixteenth Brigade, Tennessee Militia, in 1839.

William's father, John Harding, owned prosperous plantations in both Tennessee and Arkansas. In 1839, John turned over the management of Belle Meade, his magnificent plantation near

Nashville, to William. An accomplished horseman with a keen interest in thoroughbred horses, William had already proven to his father that he could successfully manage a large plantation. While managing McSpadden's Bend, another of the Harding's plantations located near Stones River in middle Tennessee, William had expanded the farm to include profitable cotton crops.

Despite his numerous accomplishments, William encountered several personal tragedies during the 1830s. His 1829 marriage to Selena McNairy produced four children, but two of the babies died during infancy. With Selena's death in 1837, William was left to raise their remaining two children, John and Nathaniel, on his own.

As a widower with two young sons, William must have been joyous when the lovely Elizabeth McGavock accepted his proposal of marriage in late 1839. On a frigid night in January 1840, William had veered a horse-drawn sleigh over the frozen, snow-covered ground, and arrived at Carnton in grand style to exchange wedding vows with Elizabeth. At the reception, the McGavocks served a "full bushel of steaming hot apple brandy toddy" to guests.

Although Elizabeth lovingly cared for her two small stepsons after her marriage to William, she longed for children of her own. Tragically, her first child was born dead in 1841. A second pregnancy three years later also ended in stillbirth. To make matters worse, Elizabeth's stepson, Nathaniel, was thrown from a horse during a visit to his grandparents' home in Nashville in 1843 and instantly killed. Now only one of William's four children with his first wife remained alive.

Finally, Elizabeth gave birth to a healthy daughter in 1846. The Hardings named their daughter Selene in memory of William's first wife. The following year, the couple rejoiced at the birth of their second daughter, Sarah Susan. But the little girl, who had been named in honor of her grandmothers, lived only nine months. Although another healthy girl, Mary Elizabeth, was born in 1850,

Elizabeth lost three more infants between 1854 and 1860. With the high rate of infant mortality during the nineteenth century, only two of the eight children born to William and Elizabeth Harding—Selene and Mary—survived infancy. And family lore contends that both daughters narrowly escaped death when they were dropped from an upstairs window onto a feather bed during a fire at Belle Meade in 1851.

Although Elizabeth struggled with health problems during her pregnancies throughout the 1840s and 1850s, she managed to garner and maintain the reputation of being a gracious hostess. Belle Meade was often the site of weddings and lavish social events, including a reception for Sarah Childress Polk, widow of former-president James K. Polk, in 1861. Since Sarah Polk rarely left her Nashville residence, Elizabeth honored the presence of the former First Lady with a grand reception at Belle Meade.

The reception was one of the last elaborate festivities held at Belle Meade before the drums of war echoed throughout Tennessee. In 1861, William was appointed to the Military and Financial Board of Tennessee, a three-man committee charged with the responsibilities of equipping an army for the South. As president of the board, William devoted most of his time to the cause and relied on Elizabeth and his overseer to manage the plantation.

Due to William's staunch support of the Confederacy, however, orders for his arrest were issued in early April 1862. Andrew Johnson, military governor of Tennessee, decided to use William as an example to other Confederate sympathizers by exiling him to prison beyond state boundaries. By April 19, William was on his way to Fort Mackinac, Michigan. During a stop in Louisville, Kentucky, William dashed off a letter to Elizabeth, assuring her that he was well in spite of his forced exile.

Elizabeth's immediate response informed her husband that many servants, family members, and friends had offered their help during his absence. In her letter, she also expressed her love and concern:

> I write as though you had been absent a month, instead of a week, and indeed you have been away a month nearly from home. How much more like a month does it seem and my very state of uncertainty, as to where you were taken to, makes the time drag heavily. I fear the cold climate of Mackinaw will not agree with your constitution, as I know it will not with your feelings.

With her husband in prison, Elizabeth assumed William's responsibilities at the plantation, overseeing daily operations of the massive estate. Each morning, she visited the slave quarters to tend to the sick and injured. Each evening, she reviewed the plantation records with James Beasley, the farm manager. She faithfully wrote letters to her husband, warning him not to trust newspaper accounts about the war and keeping him informed about numerous events at the plantation, ranging from the deaths of elderly servants to her concern for the health of his stallion.

William wrote to his wife each week from his prison quarters at Fort Mackinac. John Harding, William's father, frequently visited Belle Meade during William's imprisonment, listening intently as Elizabeth read William's latest letters to him. At the age of eighty-four, John could not understand why his son was in prison. The elderly man constantly asked, "When is he coming home, daughter?" Elizabeth confided to a friend that she wished "to God" that she had an answer to her beloved father-in-law's question.

In early June, tears sprang to Elizabeth's eyes when she received seven photographs of her husband. Murmuring that he looked pale and "not as healthful" as she had hoped, she excused herself from the room to regain her composure. She later gave away all but one of the photographs to friends and family members.

Attempting to keep life as normal as possible, Elizabeth arranged for her daughters to travel into town every other day for French and music lessons. Neighbors and friends frequently visited Belle Meade, including two friends of the Harding sisters. Although one thousand Federal troops had recently feasted on the plantation's crops, the friends reported that food was plentiful during their visit to Belle Meade and the slaves remained devoted to their owners.

Throughout the summer of 1862, Elizabeth became determined to travel to Michigan and see William, especially after she heard that Governor Johnson might be willing to grant him a parole. But each time she worked out the details of her journey, another obstacle would arise, preventing the trip. In late July, Elizabeth arranged an appointment with Governor Johnson, hoping he would finally grant her request to allow William to stay with her at a Mackinac Island hotel during her upcoming visit to Michigan. But the governor failed to keep the appointment with Elizabeth when she arrived at the state capitol with her daughters.

Dismayed, Elizabeth headed home for the night. Friends had warned her that travelers who refused to sign an oath of allegiance to the Union would be turned back, but Elizabeth never dreamed that guards would prevent her from traveling home with her daughters and their driver, Miles. An officer stopped the carriage and questioned Elizabeth at length. Elizabeth described the confrontation in a letter to William:

> An inferior officer of Johnson's precious body guard stepped up, took the "pass" from Miles and remarked to me, "I suppose you have read the oath on the back of this pass, Madam."
>
> I replied, "I have, Sir."

"Have you any objection to taking this oath?"

"I have most decidedly. . . . They are numerous and insuperable, sir, but why do you ask? My pass is correct and renewed a few days since."

He replied, "My orders are to let no one through, unless they take the oath, or have taken it."

I asked him why he did not inform people of that as they went into the city; because he had no orders to that effect, beside they were surrounded with dangers, and must be very strict with both women and men.

Just then Miles spoke up and said, "I showed Gov [ernor] Johnson my pass this evening, and asked him if it would take us home, and he said, 'Yes.'"

The man looked at me earnestly for a moment and said, "Madam, if you will give me your word, you will not give any information to any Confederate Calvary that may visit your house, tonight or tomorrow, detrimental to us?"

"I will certainly promise that, as I have no information to give."

After questioning Elizabeth's daughters, the guard allowed the party to proceed. But the ordeal only increased Elizabeth's determination to see her husband. "I will go to see you yet," she vowed in a letter to William, "but I must wait patiently until the times are more settled." The trying event also fueled her anger toward Governor Johnson. In the same letter, Elizabeth added, "'Put not your faith in Princes,' sayeth the Bible, but I have almost lost faith in all politicians and Union Governors."

With her daily responsibilities at the plantation and mounting concern over her husband, Elizabeth's worries intensified. When a Federal commander demanded that she provide twelve men with supplies to build fortifications at Nashville, Elizabeth conceded that she was so "shocked and appalled by this act of gross injustice and violence" that she temporarily gave up all hope of getting to Fort Mackinac.

Matters worsened when a former employee asked for help in returning to his home in South Carolina. Aware that her husband was fond of the man who had once worked as a jockey at Belle Meade, Elizabeth presented the man with a horse for his trip. But federal officers arrested the man before he could leave Davidson County, and Elizabeth was suspected of sending letters by the jockey to the Confederate cause. She immediately penned a letter to Governor Johnson, explaining the situation. Vouching for the man's innocence, she denied any involvement in espionage.

She was exonerated of all charges, but the turbulent events of the summer of 1862 took their toll on Elizabeth. Between the responsibilities of running the plantation, caring for ill servants, and defending her home and property, Elizabeth assumed the added responsibilities of caring for her aging father-in-law, her own widowed mother, Sarah Rodgers McGavock, and her invalid sister, Mary McGavock Southall. Concerned family members noted that an overworked Elizabeth had lost weight from fatigue and worry during the general's absence, although she never complained and had not been "in bed one hour from sickness," in spite of recurring pains in her side. "She is overburdened with care and—she shows it in her face—looks pale and careworn," Elizabeth's sister noted in a letter to William.

Ironically, the summer of 1862 was not as difficult for William, even though he was confined to prison. One of only three prisoners at Fort Mackinac, William was assigned to a private room that had recently been renovated. Guards treated him with respect, allowing him to walk on the beach for two hours each day and to attend regular chapel services.

By the end of the summer, Elizabeth relinquished the idea of visiting her husband, but the first part of September brought more problems at Belle Meade. Soldiers invaded the premises, knocking down stone walls that surrounded the plantation, stealing livestock, and taking the majority of the crops and vegetables. Elizabeth prevented the troops from taking a valuable stallion by showing them a letter from a Union commander that offered protection to Belle Meade.

Distraught by the incident, Elizabeth complained to Governor Johnson, writing a lengthy letter that detailed all of her losses and pleading that "your Excellency will do something to mitigate this monstrous evil." But Elizabeth must have temporarily set aside the matter when Governor Johnson ordered William's release from prison on September 25. A few days later, William arrived home. Under the terms of his parole, William agreed to "support the Constitution of the United States . . .[and] not to give any aid or assistance to the rebellion," including any "information to the 'enemy' which would forward their movements."

William's return to Belle Meade must have eased many of Elizabeth's burdens, but life remained difficult as the fighting continued around Nashville. During her husband's brief absence from home in the spring of 1863, Elizabeth valiantly rose to the defense of family and friends when a rowdy band of Confederates arrived on her front lawn in the wee hours of the morning. And Carnton, Elizabeth's family home, was designated as a field hospital for dying and injured soldiers. Four Confederate generals died at Carnton during a bloody battle on the grounds of the plantation in late 1864.

Difficulties hit closer to home in December 1864. During the Battle of Nashville, fighting raged across the Belle Meade lawn. For two weeks before the battle, Belle Meade became the headquarters of a Confederate general and his staff. Suspecting the Hardings of "aiding and abetting" the enemy, Federal authorities threatened to send the couple through the Confederate lines to fend for themselves. Elizabeth defended herself by writing to the authorities:

> I am called on to state the reasons why I should not be sent within the lines of the enemy. I answer because I have done nothing detrimental to the United States government from the commencement of the war to the present time, nothing whatsoever that the authorities could disapprove. Moreover, all my family ties, my kindred, and my dearest friends are here. I therefore hope I shall not be banished from my birthplace and home.

Fortunately, Elizabeth and her husband were allowed to remain in their home throughout the duration of the war. Years later, a Confederate officer who served on the general's staff at Belle Meade recalled that Elizabeth Harding was "a lady of marked character and ability. . . . She presided over that grand old home with unsurpassed eloquence, and I venture to speak for all the party when I say they were never better or more hospitably entertained."

In the years following the Civil War, Belle Meade became renowned for breeding and raising thoroughbred horses. Today, the restored Belle Meade mansion offers thousands of annual visitors with an intimate glimpse into the lives of the Harding family and the splendor of the "Queen of Tennessee Plantations."

Unfortunately, however, Elizabeth did not live to see the resurgence of her magnificent homeplace. On August 8, 1867, Elizabeth Harding died at the age of forty-eight. Although the cause of her death is unknown, Harding descendants believe that Elizabeth's devotion to the needs of others and her valiant defense of home and family during the Civil War years took precedence over her own frail health, contributing to her death at an early age.

ELIZABETH MERIWETHER GILMER

1861–1951

Columnist Dorothy Dix

$\mathcal{E}$lizabeth Gilmer addressed the envelope to her husband in Tennessee, wondering what George would say when he read her letter. Thrilled that the *Daily Picayune* had asked her to write a weekly column, she was eager to share the good news with her husband.

But deep in her heart, Elizabeth sensed George would not be pleased with her success in New Orleans. Shortly after their wedding day, she'd realized that she'd married a man with severe emotional problems. Moody and bitter, George rarely offered his support for anything she tried to do.

Now, in the spring of 1895, Elizabeth knew she had no choice but to pursue her career in journalism. The previous year, at age thirty-three, she'd accepted a job at the *Daily Picayune* out of financial necessity, since she was unable to depend on her husband for support. Despite her age and lack of formal training in journalism, the newspaper had taken notice of her work. She would be writing a weekly column under the pen name Dorothy Dix.

If Elizabeth Gilmer could have peered into a crystal ball on that day in 1895, she would have been astonished to learn the course of her future. Although she would never experience the happiness

Elizabeth Meriwether Gilmer

of a fulfilling relationship with her emotionally unstable husband, Elizabeth Meriwether Gilmer would transform herself into the all-knowing Dorothy Dix, the most revered newspaper columnist in the world during the 1930s and 1940s. Admired for her quick wit, common sense, and practical approach to life's problems, Dorothy Dix became an American legend through her newspaper columns. For more than fifty years, her words of advice consoled millions of readers while bringing fame and fortune to the Tennessee native.

Alhough her troubled marriage was far from satisfying, Elizabeth's own problems provided her with an uncanny ability to sympathize with and relate to the problems of others through her advice columns. Perhaps she best described her own philosophy of life when she penned these words:

> I have been through the depths of poverty and sickness. . . . I have known want and struggle and anxiety and despair. . . . As I look back upon my life I see it as a battle-field strewn with the wrecks of dead dreams and broken hopes and shattered illusions—a battle in which I always fought with the odds tremendously against me, and which has left me scarred and bruised and maimed and old before my time.

> But I have learned to live each day as it comes, and not to borrow trouble by dreading the morrow. It is the dark menace of the picture that makes cowards of us. I put that dread from me because experience has taught me that when the time comes that I so fear, the strength and wisdom to meet it will be given me.

Elizabeth Meriwether was born on November 18, 1861 in Montgomery County, Tennessee, near the Kentucky border. The oldest child of Maria Winston and William Douglas Meriwether, Elizabeth spent her early years at Woodstock, her family's farm. After the Civil War, financial difficulties forced the family—including Elizabeth and her younger brother and sister, Mary and Edward—to move to nearby Clarksville, Tennessee.

Maria died when Elizabeth was still a child. A widower with three young children to raise, William Meriwether married a widowed cousin, Martha Gilmer Chase. A stern disciplinarian, Martha was a strong influence on the Meriwether children—especially Elizabeth—during their teenage years.

At the Female Academy of Clarksville, Elizabeth discovered a love of writing. She graduated from the academy at age sixteen and left for Hollins Institute in Virginia. But plain-spoken, country-born Elizabeth found little joy in the fashionable school for young ladies. Although she received the school's annual composition medal—which she later claimed was "the turning point" of her life—Elizabeth returned to Clarksville after completing only one semester at Hollins.

Back at home, Elizabeth worked as a bookkeeper for her father's manufacturing company. Then, while visiting Martha's family in Quincy, Illinois, Elizabeth met her stepmother's brother, George Gilmer. Ten years older than Elizabeth, George was full of intriguing tales about his many travels and his brief residence at a western post in Indian territory. In the following months, Elizabeth became better acquainted with George during his visits to the Meriwether home in Tennessee. Martha, who thought her brother needed to settle down, highly encouraged George and Elizabeth to spend time together.

On November 21, 1882, Elizabeth and George married. George immediately went to work at William's manufacturing plant. But within a few weeks, the bride realized her groom was a restless man with unbalanced emotions. Moody and unpredictable, he sometimes vanished for days, offering no explanation for his absence when he finally returned home.

For the next few years, George jumped from job to job. Elizabeth accompanied him each time he took a new position in another Tennessee town. In her spare time, she began writing stories and sending her compositions to newspapers. By the late 1880s, her first stories appeared in the *Nashville American*.

Worries about George's erratic behavior and a lack of steady income affected Elizabeth's health during the early 1890s. Concerned about his daughter's frazzled nerves and frequent coughing spells, William took Elizabeth to Bay Saint Louis, a small Mississippi town on the Gulf Coast, for a few months of rest. While recuperating, Elizabeth met Eliza Nicholson, the owner and editor of the *Daily Picayune* in New Orleans. Impressed with Elizabeth's writing, the newspaper editor promptly purchased a story from her.

In 1894, Eliza hired Elizabeth as a full-time writer for the *Daily Picayune*. When she assumed the position at the age of thirty-three, Elizabeth had never set foot in a newspaper office, but she quickly proved to be a versatile, competent writer.

Elizabeth moved into a boarding house in New Orleans and walked to work at the newspaper offices each day. She faithfully sent part of her earnings to George, who remained at home in Tennessee, excited about a new manufacturing process he had developed for distilling turpentine.

Elizabeth initially wrote only obituaries and recipes for the paper, but she soon tackled drama reviews, society notes, and other features. And within a few months, her weekly column debuted in the newspaper. Written under the pen name of Dorothy Dix, Elizabeth's first column appeared in the *Daily Picayune* on May 5, 1895. An instant success, the weekly pieces covered a variety of topics that appealed to female readers.

To Elizabeth's surprise, readers began sending letters to her.

Impressed by the columnist's common sense and practical approach to life, they turned to her for advice on personal matters. Although Elizabeth dashed off personal replies to many letters, her columns began to address common problems of readers, using phrases like "a woman recently asked . . ." and "a letter crossed my desk . . ."

In 1897, the *Daily Picayune* sent Elizabeth to England to cover Queen Victoria's Diamond Jubilee. Although George stayed home with his new manufacturing business, Elizabeth's father accompanied her on the three-month journey. Her published reports about the trip became immensely popular, paving the way for more exciting assignments from the newspaper.

By the turn of the century, Elizabeth's weekly column had been picked up by other newspapers, which increased her popularity and name recognition as a columnist.

Soon she was receiving invitations to speak to women's groups. She began to use the name Dorothy Dix instead of her own.

As her work attracted national attention, the editor of the *New York Journal* asked Elizabeth in 1901 to report on the activities of Carrie Nation on special assignment. The columnist tracked down the prohibition leader in Kansas. Elizabeth—now well-established as Dorothy Dix—wrote and submitted the piece and then returned to New Orleans to resume her position at the *Daily Picayune.*

Impressed with Dorothy's article, the *New York Journal* promptly offered her a full-time position at an annual salary of five thousand dollars. The staggering offer stunned Dorothy. Not even the governor of Louisiana earned five thousand dollars per year. She accepted the offer on the condition that she would continue her weekly columns for the *Picayune* and moved to New York to start working at William Randolph Hearst's *New York Journal* on April 1, 1901.

Beginning with her very first assignment, Dorothy made a name for herself at the *Journal* as a crime reporter. Her sympathetic nature put people at ease and encouraged them to talk freely about their situations. Writing with clarity and freshness, Dorothy covered the most sensational murder cases of the era. By 1902, she was hailed as one of the top journalists of the day.

All the while, she continued to write her columns. With her extraordinary empathy for the problems of others, Dorothy Dix's popularity continued to increase. Streams of letters from readers poured into the *Journal*, requesting Dorothy's advice. By 1905, her column had become a daily feature of the Hearst newspaper syndicate. Along the way, Dorothy's salary increased to thirteen thousand dollars per year. To celebrate, she purchased a car and rented a lovely New York apartment.

But as her career skyrocketed, her marriage continued to flounder. George eventually joined Dorothy in New York, but he openly resented his wife's success and fame. Suffering from arthritis and recurring headaches, he rarely appeared in public with his well-known wife.

Concentrating on her work, Dorothy became an active supporter of the women's suffrage movement. In her columns, she constantly advocated financial independence for women, undoubtedly a reflection of her own personal situation. Her advice to the lovelorn attracted the most attention from readers. With the advent of World War I, young couples often asked Dorothy Dix: Should we marry now or wait?

By the middle of the 1910s, Dorothy's daily column appeared in more than one hundred newspapers across the county. Collections of her columns were published in books. Major women's magazines, such as *Good Housekeeping*, often carried her byline. Ministers quoted her from their pulpits, doctors dispensed her columns as substitutes for pills, and companies quoted her witty sayings in their advertisements.

Dorothy's popularity continued to soar, even after she left the *New York Journal*. Weary of crime reporting in addition to her column responsibilities, Dorothy accepted an offer in 1917 from the Wheeler Newspaper Syndicate. Working from home, she concentrated solely on writing advice columns. At the same time, she took care of George, whose failing health needed her attention.

Although George's physical health improved after the couple traveled to the Far East and stayed in Saratoga Springs for several months, his black moods and raging tempers continued. Bitter and resentful of his wife's success, he moved to Florida during the early 1920s.

Hurt and disillusioned, Dorothy left New York and returned to New Orleans. Devoting all her time to her work, she launched a new question-and-answer format for her columns and continued to win the hearts of readers with her sound advice and humorous sayings. By the time a rival syndicate lured her away from Wheeler, Dorothy's income exceeded seventy-five thousand dollars per year.

To honor her achievements, Tulane University awarded Dorothy an honorary degree in 1927. The following year, thousands of fans flocked to a local park when the city of New Orleans celebrated "Dorothy Dix Day" in June 1928. Three years later, Dorothy received a second honorary degree from Oglethorpe University.

George, however, continued to haunt Dorothy until his death in 1929. With the decline of his mental and physical health, he had been hospitalized by his family and spent the last days of his life in a mental institution.

Though Dorothy grieved for the loss of her estranged husband, her work gave focus and meaning to her life. By the 1930s, she was receiving four to five hundred letters each day. Employing a full-time secretary, Dorothy frequently sent personal replies to readers and prepared months of columns in advance. Along with a rigorous writing schedule for her daily columns, she managed to publish seven books by 1939. Still, she took time to enjoy her success, frequently traveling to foreign countries such as Tahiti, Australia, and the Philippines.

In 1938, a publishing survey revealed that Dorothy Dix's column held the distinction of being the oldest column in the newspaper industry. No other column had continuously appeared in print longer than Dorothy's. At the time, more than two hundred newspapers featured the daily column of the remarkable Dorothy Dix, who celebrated her seventy-seventh birthday in late 1938.

With the approach of World War II, Dorothy's advice reflected timeless values in a changing era. She advised aging readers to keep a "limber mind" even though "we can't keep our joints from getting stiff." And she cautioned soldiers not to "rush into marriage because some girl weeps on your shoulder and tells you how much she loves you."

After nearly twenty years with the Ledger Syndicate, Dorothy signed a new contract with another syndicate in 1942, at the age of eighty-one. Earning more than ninety thousand dollars per year, Dorothy lived alone and maintained a sharpness of mind that amazed her friends, family, and fans.

By the late 1940s, however, work became more difficult as Dorothy's hearing dimmed and sight diminished. She wrote her last column in 1949. At that time, the syndicate pulled previous columns from their files and reprinted Dorothy Dix's advice for millions of readers. Many insisted her counsel seemed as fresh and appropriate as ever, even though much of the advice had been written for previous generations of readers.

In the spring of 1950, Dorothy suffered a stroke, requiring hospitalization. On December 16, 1951, the acclaimed journalist died of kidney failure in New Orleans at the age of ninety. After private funeral services, she was buried in New Orleans.

At the end of Dorothy Dix's glorious career, nearly three hundred newspapers across the globe were delivering her column to an estimated sixty million readers each day. At the time of her death, she was America's highest paid and most widely read female journalist—achieving success by dispensing practical advice to the world through her newspaper column for more than half a century.

Miss Dix's Dictates for a Happy Life

During World War II, one of Dorothy's most requested columns was her Ten Rules for Happiness.

First. Make up your mind to be happy. Happiness is largely a matter of self-hypnotism. You can think yourself happy or you can think yourself miserable. It is up to you . . . learn to find pleasure in simple things. If you can't go to the opera, you can turn on the radio. Nail on your face the smile that won't come off, and after a bit you will find that it comes naturally.

Second. Make the best of your lot. Of course, you're not everything you want and things are not just right. Nobody is that lucky. Even the most fortunate have a lot of crumpled rose leaves under their forty mattresses of ease. There isn't a single human being who hasn't plenty to cry over, and the trick is to make the laughs outweigh the tears.

Third. Don't take yourself too seriously. Don't think that everything that happens to you is of world-shaking importance and that somehow you should have been protected from the misfortunes that befall other people. When death robs you of one you love, or you lose your job, don't demand to know of high heaven why this should happen to you and grow rebellious and morbid over your sorrow. We are never happy until we learn to laugh at ourselves.

Fourth. Don't take other people too seriously. They are not so much, anyway. Don't let their criticisms worry you. You can't please everybody, so please yourself. Don't let your neighbors set your standards for you. Don't run into debt trying to keep up with the Joneses, or bore yourself to death trying to be as intelligent as the Highbrows. Be yourself and do the things you enjoy doing if you want to be comfortable and happy.

Fifth. Don't borrow trouble. You have to pay compound interest on that and it will bankrupt you in the end. It is a queer thing, but imaginary troubles are harder to bear than actual ones. There are none of us who have not lain awake at night petrified with dread of some calamity that we feared might befall us and that we felt would shatter our lives if it should occur. Generally it never happened, but if it did, it was not so bad after all and we survived it without serious injury. Enjoy today and let tomorrow take care of itself. There is no sounder adage than that which bids us not to trouble trouble until trouble troubles us. The only good that worrying ever did anyone was make him thin. It is grand for the figure but hard on the disposition.

Sixth. Don't cherish enmities and grudges. Don't keep up old quarrels. Don't remember all the mean things people have done to you. Forget them. Hate is a dreadful chemical that we distill in our own hearts, that poisons our own souls. It takes all the joy out of life and hurts us far worse than it does anyone else. There is nothing so depressing as having a grudge against someone. Nothing makes a home so miserable as for the family not to be on good terms. Meeting someone you don't speak to will spoil any party. So if you have an enemy, forgive him and kiss on both cheeks, not for his sake but simply because it is making you too unhappy and uncomfortable to be stirred up in wrath against him.

Seventh. Keep in circulation. Go around and meet people. Belong to clubs. Travel as much as you can. Have as many interests as possible. Have hosts of friends. That is the way to keep yourself cheerful and jolly and thinking that this is the best of all possible worlds.

Eighth. Don't hold post-mortems. Don't spend your life brooding over the mistakes you have made or the sorrows that have befallen on you. What is done is done and cannot be changed, but you can have your whole future life in which to make good. Not all the tears can bring back those we have lost, but we can make life miserable for ourselves and those about us by our unavailing weeping. Quit beating upon your breast because you haven't as much money as you used to have. Don't be one of those who never get over things. Have the courage to take misfortune on the chin and come up smiling.

Ninth. Do something for somebody less fortunate than yourself. Minister to other people's trouble and you will forget your own. Happiness is a coin that we keep only when we give it away.

Tenth. Keep busy. That is the sovereign remedy for unhappiness. Hard work is a panacea for trouble. You never saw a very busy person who was unhappy.

IDA B. WELLS BARNETT

1862–1931

Investigative Journalist and Social Reformer

The Memphis train station bustled with activity as an attractive black woman stepped up to the ticket counter and purchased a first-class ticket for Woodstock, a rural community in Shelby County, Tennessee. Ready to begin the short journey to her teaching job at a small Woodstock school on that bright May morning in 1884, the woman picked up her long skirts and boarded the train.

As Ida B. Wells slipped into the first-class coach reserved for white ladies, she ignored the whispers and stares swirling around her. Holding her head high, the twenty-two-year-old teacher settled into a seat just as the conductor hurried down the aisle and stopped beside her.

Black women were not allowed to sit in the first-class coach, the conductor announced. Ida would have to move to the second-class smoking car and travel with the rest of the black passengers on the train. Ida refused to vacate her seat. After all, she'd purchased a ticket for first-class accommodations. Wasn't she entitled to ride in the first-class car?

Ida B. Wells Barnett

Ignoring her protests, the conductor reached out and grabbed her arm. Resisting his attempt to physically remove her from the seat, Ida sank her teeth into his hand. A baggage man leaped to assist the conductor, and the two men dragged the defiant young woman from the train while the remaining passengers applauded and cheered.

Infuriated by the humiliating experience, Ida hired a lawyer and filed a discrimination lawsuit against the Chesapeake, Ohio and Southwestern Railroad Company, owner of the railway line. Ida's attorney contended that the railroad had violated "separate but equal" laws by failing to provide blacks with accommodations that were "equal" to the facilities for whites.

In December 1885, the Memphis circuit court ruled in Ida's favor with a five-hundred-dollar settlement. Three years later, how- ever, Tennessee's Supreme Court reversed the decision and charged the court costs to Ida.

To express her outrage at the verdict, Ida penned a series of newspaper articles describing the railroad incident and encouraging African Americans to defend their rights for equality. Reprints of the articles soon appeared in other newspapers, establishing Ida as an outspoken critic against racism and discrimination.

With her popular writing, Ida launched a new career as a jour- nalist. At the same time, she embarked on a life-long campaign to improve conditions for black Americans. One of the first black women to work as an investigative reporter, Ida B. Wells became a crusader for equal rights.

Ironically, more than seventy years after Ida's encounter with the train conductor, another black woman, Rosa Parks, experienced a remarkably similar situation. Rosa's refusal to relinquish her seat to a white man on a crowded bus in Montgomery, Alabama, in 1955 launched the civil rights movement of the 1950s.

For more than four decades, Ida's compelling articles and persuasive speeches informed the world about grave injustices against blacks, particularly the many instances of lynching in the South during the late 1800s and the early 1900s. Throughout the remainder of her life, she worked tirelessly to promote justice for blacks, personally investigating inequities and organizing human rights groups to support her causes.

The eldest of eight children, Ida B. Wells was born into slavery on July 16, 1862 in Holly Springs, Mississippi. Six months after her birth, the Emancipation Proclamation granted freedom to Ida and her parents, Elizabeth Warrenton and James Wells.

During Ida's childhood, the Wells family sought to improve the quality of their lives through education and civic activities. Ida attended Shaw University in Holly Springs. This Methodist institution, established in 1866, provided educational opportunities for both elementary and advanced students. In later years, the school became known as Rust College. Her father James, a skilled carpenter who actively participated in civic activities in their small Mississippi community, served as a member of the first board of trustees at Shaw University. Elizabeth, a former slave from Virginia, attended the local school with her children so she could learn to read and write.

The Wells household suffered a series of tragedies during the 1870s. Not long after the death of one of the Wells's sons from spinal meningitis, an epidemic of yellow fever swept through the little town of Holly Springs. The fever claimed the lives of both Ida's parents and her youngest brother, leaving sixteen-year-old Ida with the responsibility of raising her siblings.

To support her three sisters and two remaining brothers, Ida studied for the Mississippi teachers' examination. After passing the test, she accepted a teaching position for twenty-five dollars per month at a one-room school for blacks in rural Holly Springs.

Unable to resist an opportunity to improve her lot in life, Ida accepted an aunt's invitation to move to Memphis with two of her sisters in the early 1880s. After securing apprenticeships for her three other siblings and arranging with relatives for their care, Ida packed her meager belongings and headed for Memphis.

The ambitious young woman diligently prepared for the examination to obtain a teaching license, as required by Negro Public Schools in Memphis, in hopes of obtaining a job in the city's school system. She attended summer sessions at Nashville's Fisk University to further her education at the same time. Throughout the school year, she taught in the rural Shelby County town of Woodstock.

The daily train commute between Memphis and Woodstock became routine for Ida, who usually sat in the smoking car until the fateful May day in 1884 when she was physically removed from the whites-only car reserved for white women. When Ida initially won her lawsuit against the railroad in the Memphis court only to have the decision overruled by the Tennessee Supreme Court in 1887, she noted in her diary:

> I felt so disappointed because I had hoped such great things from my suit for my people generally. I firmly believed all along that the law was on our side and would, when we appealed to it, give us justice. . . . If it were possible, I would gather my race in my arms and fly away with them. O God, is there no redress, no peace, no justice in this land for us? Thou hast always fought the battles of the weak and oppressed. Come to my aid this moment and teach me what to do, for I am sorely, bitterly, disappointed.

Ida passed the teachers exam required by the black school system of Memphis and obtained a teaching position in the city during 1884, eliminating the need for the daily train ride to Woodstock. Still teaching in Memphis at the time of the Tennessee Supreme

Court's ruling in 1887, she channeled her disappointment over losing the case into a newspaper article about her experiences. Written under the pen name "Iola," the article appeared in *Living Way*, a religious weekly for African Americans, in 1887.

Soon Ida was contributing articles to other black publications throughout the country, including *New York Age* and *Indianapolis World*. By 1889, she had saved enough money from her teaching job to become the editor and part-owner of the *Free Speech and Headlight*, a Memphis newspaper that served the black community.

Ida's scathing editorials on the pages of the *Free Speech and Headlight* constantly denounced racism and discrimination, generating heated debate in the community. As a direct result of an editorial that criticized the local school board's failure to provide segregated Negro schools with the same resources as white facilities, the Memphis school system dismissed Ida from her teaching job in 1891.

Undaunted, Ida pressed on, continuing to publish articles and editorials that condemned injustices toward blacks. She specifically focused on the crime of lynching in her editorials after three black businessmen were lynched in Memphis on March 9, 1892.

The troubling incident began when the trio of young blacks opened a grocery store across the street from an existing store operated by whites. Furious that the new store was luring away their customers, the white competitors formed a lynch mob and prepared to attack the black businessmen and their supporters.

Blacks in the community received advanced warning of the attack. Banding together, they armed themselves for the onslaught. But as the white mob descended upon the store and destroyed the facility, thirty-one blacks were arrested and unjustly charged with conspiracy. The arrests did not satisfy the white mob. Nine white men dragged the three store owners from the Memphis jail, then shot and hanged the black men in a vacant lot near the railroad tracks.

For the next three months, Ida condemned the atrocious crimes in her *Free Speech and Headlight* editorials, insisting that the city's white public officials not only tolerated but encouraged the lynchings. Demanding that the murderers be brought to justice, she wrote, "We ask this in the name of God and in the name of the law we have always obeyed and upheld and intend to uphold and obey in the future." Ida also encouraged readers to boycott city streetcars or to leave Memphis until the murderers received punishment for their crimes. Taking her advice, hundreds of blacks fled the city. At the same time, she researched previous lynching cases and reported her findings in a *Free Speech* editorial, "Eight Negroes Lynched Since Last Issue." The piece concluded that whites frequently filed false charges of rape against many lynching victims: rape was a convenient excuse to lynch blacks who had committed petty crimes.

The editorial hit the streets while Ida was attending the African Methodist Episcopal General Church Conference in Philadelphia. Enraged by the editorial, white citizens broke into the newspaper offices during her absence from the city, destroyed the presses, and burned the remaining copies of the issue. The angry mob also threatened to lynch Ida if she returned to Memphis.

Receiving word of the threat, Ida did not return to Memphis or the South. She relocated to New York and joined the staff of *New York Age* as a columnist. She persisted in her battle against racial injustice and lynching through her writings. In her autobiography she wrote: "Having lost my paper, had a price put on my life, and been made an exile from home for hinting at the truth, I felt that I owed it to myself and to my race to tell the whole truth now that I was where I could do so freely."

Spreading the word about the atrocities of lynching became a personal crusade for the young woman. In the preface of her article, "Southern Horrors: Lynch Law in all its Phases," Ida stated, "Somebody must show that the Afro-American race is sinned against [rather] than sinning, and it seems to have fallen upon me to do so."

First published in October 1892 and later reprinted as a brochure, the article received national attention and prompted scores of public speaking engagements for Ida. An articulate and effective speaker, she traveled to Europe and presented a series of lectures on lynching throughout England, Scotland, and Wales. An entry in her diary noted the demand for her appearances during her European tour:

> I have spoken not less than thirty-five times at different gatherings of different sorts during my six weeks' stay in London and find more and more invitations than I can fill from people who are anxious to know the facts. Again I cannot help wishing that our own people would give the same opportunity for open discussion on this subject. In no other way can it be conquered save to meet it fairly.

Both at home and abroad, Ida became the leader of an international anti-lynching campaign, garnering praise for her efforts from influential individuals such as Susan B. Anthony and Frederick Douglas. Following two speaking tours in Europe, Ida returned to the United States to continue her campaign against discrimination, injustice, and Southern lynching.

Soon after settling in Chicago, she noticed and protested the exclusion of blacks from the Columbian Exposition, an international event held in Chicago during 1893. Voicing her opposition to the lack of black representation, she wrote, published, and distributed the booklet, "The Reason Why the Colored American is Not in the World's Columbian Exposition."

The subject of lynching remained a personal crusade for Ida. She frequently investigated the cause of lynchings, traveling to crime

IDA B. WELLS BARNETT

sites to interview eyewitnesses. She discovered that an average of one hundred lynchings occurred each year throughout the 1880s and the first half of the 1890s.

In 1895, she compiled her findings in the first statistical report on lynching, *A Red Record: Tabulated Statistics and Alleged Causes of Lynching in the United States*. The one-hundred-page report eventually forced the federal government to acknowledge the crime of lynching. White government officials, however, were reluctant to penalize lynchers for their crimes. Although the first punishments for lynching were not rendered until 1918, Ida's research and published reports paved the way for the elimination of lynching in American society.

Romance entered into Ida's life in 1895 when she became engaged to attorney Ferdinand L. Barnett, founder and editor of the *Chicago Conservator*. Ida canceled the wedding ceremony on three occasions, each time to deliver an urgent address on social injustices, but the couple finally married on June 27, 1895. Ida and Ferdinand eventually became the parents of four children: Charles, Herman, Ida, and Alfreda.

Marriage and motherhood did not deter Ida from her crusade for justice and equality for blacks. During the 1890s, she organized the Ida B. Wells Women's Club, which established the first kindergarten for blacks in the city. An active member of the National Association of Colored Women, Ida became one of two black women to serve as founding members of the National Association for the Advancement of Colored People (NAACP) in 1907. And after discovering that black males were excluded from the Young Men's Christian Association (YMCA), she organized Chicago's Negro Fellowship League in 1910 to provide lodging, employment counseling, and social activities for young black men.

The suffrage movement also received Ida's attention during the first part of the twentieth century. In 1913, she founded Chicago's

Alpha Suffrage Club, the first suffrage organization in the city. As president of the group, Ida represented the club in March of 1913 at a suffrage parade sponsored by the National American Woman's Suffrage Association (NAWSA) in Washington, D.C. True to form, Ida rejected less-than-equal status among fellow suffragettes in the nation's capital. When the organizer of the march asked black women to walk at the end of the parade line, Ida refused, claiming she'd march under the Illinois state banner or not at all. As the parade started, she disappeared into the crowd of onlookers. Then, as the Chicago delegation rounded a corner, Ida slipped into line between two white women and completed the parade alongside her fellow suffragettes from Illinois.

As she grew older, Ida remained actively involved in numerous organizations and civic groups, promoting human rights and equal justice for all people. She also encouraged African Americans to take an active part in politics, running as an independent candidate for the Illinois state senate in 1930. Although defeated in the election, Ida inspired other blacks to seek political office. And she continued her battle against injustice until she died from a kidney disease on March 25, 1931, at her Chicago home.

To commemorate her accomplishments as an investigative journalist and human rights activist, the United States Postal Service issued a stamp in honor of Ida B. Wells Barnett in 1990. Five years later, the city of Chicago also honored her memory by designating the home that she shared with her husband as a Chicago landmark.

Today, many historians cite Ida's efforts as the single most important factor leading to the demise of lynching. Without Ida's courage and relentless crusade to expose the horrors of lynching, many more African Americans might have been brutally murdered at the hands of lynch mobs during the early years of the twentieth century. Her persistent defense of the rights of African Americans served as an inspiration for future generations who continued to wage the battle against discrimination in America.

EMMA BELL MILES

1879–1919

Artist, Writer, and Poet

$\mathcal{E}$mma Bell Miles stared in disbelief at the letter in her hand, astonished that anyone would take the time to praise her published poems. Savoring the kind words, she sank into a chair on the porch of her mountain cabin.

The letter was from Anna Ricketson, a prominent drama and music critic from New England, who applauded one of Emma's poems published in the *Century*. As Emma re-read Anna's message on that day in 1906, the kind words offered hope and encouragement to the talented writer and artist.

Emma lived with her husband and children in the remote mountain community of Walden's Ridge near Chattanooga, Tennessee and often felt a sense of isolation. Now, knowing her work had touched someone who lived in a far more sophisticated culture, Emma felt a wondrous sense of accomplishment. She picked up a pen and paper and wrote a response to the letter: "It meant so much to me to receive a message right out of the heart of that land of literary traditions and great names, from one so intimately connected with both. You know it is quite different here in the mountains, where the traditions . . . are, so far, anything but literary."

Emma Bell Miles

During the early part of the twentieth century, Emma Bell Miles desperately tried to support her mountain family through literary and artistic pursuits. From her home in a remote area of Tennessee, she longed to be accepted by a more sophisticated society that would fully value her immense talent. Writing about the culture of mountain people, Emma found outlets for her work with some of the nation's most prestigious publications of the day, including *Lippincott's*, *Harper's*, and *Putnam's*, but publication was bittersweet for the talented writer. Destined to live within a mountain culture that she once described as a "life sentence at hard labor," Emma never fully received the fame or fortune that she desired.

Emma Bell Miles was born on October 19, 1879 in Evansville, Indiana, the only surviving child of Benjamin Franklin Bell and Martha Ann Mirick Bell. Her twin brother, Elmer, died the day after his birth. About one year after Emma's birth, the family moved to the small town of Rabbit Hash, Kentucky, where Mr. and Mrs. Bell accepted teaching positions at the local school. A fragile child, Emma was frequently ill during her early years. Hoping a milder climate would benefit their daughter, the Bells packed up their belongings and headed south to Tennessee around 1888. The family lived at the foot of Walden's Ridge near Chattanooga for about three years then moved into a two-story frame house that Emma's father had built on a plot of land at the top of Walden's Ridge. This area is now known as Signal Mountain.

During Emma's youth on Walden's Ridge, she became an avid reader and art lover. As a teenager, she studied art reproductions at a Chattanooga department store, often lingering for hours in front of the art displays. Determined to become an artist, she saved one dollar to pay for art lessons. Then she boldly approached a local art teacher and requested one dollar's worth of lessons.

But the world of art was only one of Emma's growing interests during her teen years. A young man by the name of G. Frank Miles, a descendent of one of the first settlers on Walden's Ridge, captivated Emma's attention. During trips to Chattanooga, Emma became acquainted with Frank, the driver of a public hack that carried passengers between the ridge and the city. Emma's parents strongly opposed her interest in the uneducated mountain man.

In spite of her attraction to the mountain resident, Emma did not resist the opportunity to attend art school in Missouri when some wealthy family friends offered to pay for Emma's art instruction. Emma left Walden's Ridge at age eighteen in hopes of developing her natural talents at a St. Louis art school. But separated from family and friends, the aspiring artist developed a case of homesickness. After only one year of study, she returned to her mountain home—and Frank Miles.

Following an engagement of more than two years, Emma married Frank on October 30, 1901. She soon discovered why her parents had objected to the marriage. Frank drifted from job to job, rarely obtaining regular work and frequently complaining of health problems. With Frank's inability to provide a steady income, financial problems plagued the young newlyweds.

Struggling to survive, Emma accepted a teaching position at the Log Church School on Walden's Ridge. At the same time, she began writing poems and essays about her mountain world. To Emma's delight, one of her poems was accepted for publication in 1904.

The following year, Emma's first book was published by James Pott and Company of New York. Illustrated with Emma's paintings of mountain scenes and characters, *The Spirit of the Mountains* explored the music, traditions, culture, and daily life of mountain people. Through her eloquent writing style, she vividly described a typical day in a mountain cabin and a rural school, relationships between family members and neighbors, and sketches of mountain residents. She also provided insight on the strength and endurance of mountain people and the love they had for their land, as shown in the following excerpt:

> Solitude is deep water, and small boats do not ride well in it. Only a superficial observer could fail to understand that the mountain people really love their wilderness— love it for its beauty, its freedom. Their intimacy with it dates from a babyhood when the thrill of clean wet sand was good to little feet; when "frog-houses" were built, and little tracks were printed in rows all over the shore of the creek; when the beginnings of aesthetic feeling found expression in necklaces of scarlet haws and headdresses pinned and braided together of oak leaves, cardinal flowers and fern.

> I once rode up the [mountain] Side with a grandmother from Sawyers' Springs, who cried out, as the overhanging curve of the bluff, crowned with pines, came into view: "Now, ain't that finer than any picter you ever seed in your life? And they call us pore mountaineers! We git more out o' life than anybody."

> The charm and mystery of bygone days broods over the mountain country—the charm of pioneer hardihood, of primitive peace, of the fatalism of ancient peoples, of the rites and legends of the aborigines. To one who understands these high solitudes it is no marvel that the inhabitants should be mystics, dreamers, given to fancies often absurd, but often wildly sweet.

> Nothing less than the charm of their stern motherland could hold them here. . . . Occasionally a whole starved-out family will emigrate westward, and, having settled,

will spend years in simply waiting for a chance to sell out and move back again. All alike cling to the ungracious acres they have so patiently and hardly won, because of the wild world that lies outside their puny fences, because of the dream-vistas, blue and violet, that lead their eyes afar among the hills.

Not even the joy of publishing a book could ease Emma's troubles at home. The letter of praise from the New England critic ignited a brief spark of hope for Emma after the 1906 publication of her poem in the *Century*, but a growing family quickly brought more financial trouble to the Miles's mountain cabin. After the birth of twin daughters, Jean and Judith, Emma delivered three more babies: Joe, Kittie, and Mark. Little Mark died shortly before his fifth birthday. Years later, Emma reflected in her diary: "The pinch of utter abject poverty became harder and harder until, as the children's demands grew with their growth, its misery and shame grew insupportable."

In a desperate struggle for survival, Emma painted anything that she could sell to anyone. Keeping her expenses to a minimum, she cut her hair to make her own brushes and used water colors instead of expensive oils. She painted postcards and miniature landscapes for the summer tourists on Walden's Ridge while providing water colors for wealthy Chattanooga residents. Concentrating on her artistic talents to support the family, she temporarily abandoned her literary endeavors.

Emma found little satisfaction in painting solely for monetary reasons, but she could not afford to pursue more artistic avenues. On one occasion, she referred to her work as "those wretched little daubs of souvenirs." And an entry in her journal reveals that on a rainy summer day in 1912 she painted "fourteen of those confounded . . . little landscapes."

Prominent citizens of Chattanooga admired her work, displaying her paintings in their homes and commissioning her to paint portraits and wall murals. But Emma knew the cultured, sophisticated Chattanoogans were exploiting her talents. In one instance, she worked for three weeks to decorate a parlor and received seven dollars for her efforts.

Depending on the intellectual world for an income while living in the midst of poverty frustrated the talented artist. By 1912, Emma's anxieties intensified as her rocky marriage began to crumble. Life became an endless round of separations and reunions as Emma bounced between her and Frank's cabin and rooms that she rented in the city. Sometimes the children stayed in town with their mother; on other occasions, they remained on Walden's Ridge with Frank.

Life seemed more promising when Emma obtained a position at the *Chattanooga News* in the spring of 1914. Moving into the city, she rented a room at a boarding house for women and joined the society department of the newspaper. On May 25, 1914, she wrote in her diary:

> My position on the News enables me to come in touch with large and vital issues.... This position is one which to others seems underpaid and insignificant, but it allows me to express myself, and with some hours of extra outside work which I do as I can, the pay of $9 a week permits us to live. So it looks like a heaven-sent opportunity to me.

Thrilled with the opportunity to write for the paper, Emma discussed a variety of issues in her column, "Fountain Square Conversations." Named after Fountain Square, a Chattanooga landmark situated across the street from her boarding house, the column featured topics ranging from the plight of the country woman to the true nature of happiness.

While working at the newspaper, Emma lived in town during the week. On weekends, she returned to the family's cabin on Walden's Ridge. To her surprise, she enjoyed the brief visits with Frank and the children. In early June, she revealed in her diary: "It is simply delightful, visiting one's own home like this, and they seem to get along nearly as well without me."

Between April 3 and June 30, 1914, thirty-four of Emma's columns appeared in the *Chattanooga News*, but Emma's joyful, fulfilling experience of working for the newspaper vanished at the end of June. Illness forced her to return to her isolated life on Walden's Ridge with Frank. Despondent, Emma wrote in her diary on July 24, 1914: "All is lost now, my hope, my health, all sacrificed to a man's pleasure. This is the destiny of women under the laws and customs of our mad and cruel civilization. God deliver my daughters from such love as has ruined me. Since I left town about a month ago, I have been too ill to earn a cent."

At the time of her diary entry, Emma did not realize that pregnancy was the reason for her poor health. After a miscarriage and a hospital stay in early August, she rested at a friend's home for two weeks before returning to Walden's Ridge. For a brief time, she hoped to pay for her hospital bill of fifteen dollars by returning to her job at the newspaper, but her hopes were dashed when her husband insisted that she remain at home to fully regain her strength. Her diary entries continue to reveal her frustrations: "Looking forward to going back to work at the News to pay off the hospital bill, but this Frank positively refuses to let me do. So I am back in the same old trap, worse off and more helpless."

Life improved temporarily in the fall of 1914. Frank and Emma sold their cabin and rented a three-room apartment above a vacant store in Chattanooga. Emma sold a few sketches, while Frank earned some money from jury duty and won a "gray jenny," or female donkey, in a raffle.

But Emma's health continued to deteriorate. Diagnosed with tuberculosis, she entered a local sanatorium, Pine Breeze, in February 1915. By spring, she and her family had returned to Walden's Ridge.

Living in a mountain cabin once again, Emma faced a bleak future. Still, she pursued her artistic talents to earn money for the basic necessities of life. Though weak from her illness, she occasionally sold poems to the local newspaper. She also compiled booklets of her poems and again painted watercolors and postcards to sell to wealthy summer tourists.

During the spring and fall of 1915, Emma focused her efforts on sketching and painting birds. A nature lover who could distinguish types of birds by their individual sounds, she devoted hours to observing her subjects and bringing them to life on paper and canvas. Inspired by the popularity of her bird paintings, Emma began to dream of writing a children's book about birds.

For the next three years, Emma worked on the book while fighting her battles against poverty and tuberculosis. When the family moved to a tarpaper shack, Emma lined the walls of the main room with newspapers during the winter of 1916, "adding greatly to its comfort, light, and cleanliness," she revealed in letter to a friend. Following a popular treatment for tuberculosis that advocated fresh air, she often slept outdoors beneath a tent. Many of the sketches for her book were drawn as she rested inside the tent, using a pair of opera glasses to observe her subject matter.

Between admissions to the sanatorium, Emma finalized plans for her book. She diligently wrote text to accompany her paintings, categorizing birds by their seasonal appearances in the southern states. Since the study of birds was a regular part of school curriculums in the early decades of the twentieth century, Emma intended for the book to be used as a school textbook.

By 1918, Emma had located a publisher for her work. Weakened by tuberculosis, she dictated her final notes while confined to bed from the disease. Emma died on May 20, 1919, several weeks before the publication of her book, *Our Southern Birds*. After funeral services at Chattanooga's Christ Episcopal Church, Emma was buried in the city's White Oak Cemetery, located at the base of Walden's Ridge.

Just as Emma had envisioned, *Our Southern Birds* was eventually used as a nature textbook in Kentucky schools. When the Walden's Ridge Historical Society reprinted the book in 1984, a Chattanooga newspaper reported, "It is the artistry of Emma Bell Miles, undiminished by the passage of years, that gives [the book] continued life and interest."

Literary reviewers evidently ignored the publication of Emma's book, *The Spirit of the Mountains*, in 1905. Today, historians claim that reviews of the book cannot be found. But seventy years after the book's initial publication, a new generation of readers discovered the hidden talents of Emma Bell Miles. After the University of Tennessee Press reprinted *The Spirit of the Mountains* in 1975, state historian Wilma Dykeman lauded the book as a "landmark work of Southern literary realism and original insight and interpretation." Undoubtedly, author Emma Bell Miles would have cherished the tribute to her work.

EMMA ROCHELLE WHEELER

1882–1957

Physician and Hospital Founder

*T*he young girl clutched her father's hand as she entered the doctor's office in Gainesville, Florida. Barely six years old, little Emma Rochelle wondered if anyone could successfully treat the eye problem that had plagued her for days. A few moments later, Emma was amazed to discover that her doctor was not what she expected. To her surprise, the doctor was a woman.

At the end of the nineteenth century, the unusual experience of being treated by a female physician made a lasting impression on the young African American. Years later, Emma recalled: "Back in 1888, a little Florida farm girl with eye trouble was taken to a doctor who turned out to be the prettiest little white lady I ever saw—and I made up my mind then and there I was going to be a doctor, too."

Profoundly impressed by the female physician's successful treatment of her eye condition, Emma Rochelle pursued her dream of becoming a doctor. In the following years, she not only achieved her goal but became a trailblazer in the medical field. A practicing physician for more than fifty years, Emma established a hospital for African Americans in Tennessee, founded a nursing school, and

Emma Rochelle Wheeler

advocated pre-paid hospitalization plans. Throughout her life-time, Emma Rochelle Wheeler served the black community by working tirelessly to improve medical treatment for her fellow African Americans.

The daughter of a farmer and veterinarian, Emma was born on February 7, 1882, near Gainesville, Florida. With her father's popularity as a local veterinarian, Emma grew up in a prosperous household, along with one brother, William, and one sister, Ella. The attractive female physician who treated Emma's eye condition took a strong interest in her young patient. Throughout Emma's childhood, the physician maintained contact with Emma. And when her former patient became a student at Cookman Institute in Jacksonville, Florida, the physician frequently visited the bright young girl.

Emma completed her studies at Cookman in 1899. The fol-lowing year she became the wife of a teacher, Joseph R. Howard. Sadly, Joseph died of typhoid fever in 1901, passing away before the birth of his son, Joseph, Jr.

Soon after Joseph's death, Emma and her infant son moved to Nashville, Tennessee. Continuing the pursuit of her dream of be-coming a doctor, Emma enrolled in the medical college of Walden University. In 1905, Emma received her medical degree from Walden University's Meharry Medical, Dental, and Pharmaceutical College. During the week of Meharry's commencement, she married a fel-low classmate, Dr. John N. Wheeler. The wedding ceremony was held on February 28, 1905 in the Meharry auditorium.

Immediately after graduation from medical school, Emma and John moved to Chattanooga and established a joint medical practice on Main Street. Practicing medicine together for the next ten years, the couple became acutely aware of the need for better hospital facilities for their African-American patients. Although blacks com-prised more than one-third of Chattanooga's population at the turn of the century, hospital care for African Americans was woefully inadequate. Black patients at the city's white hospital were restricted to beds in the black ward, located in the basement of the facility.

Emma dreamed of a facility that would treat African American patients with the respect and care that they deserved. She also envisioned a hospital that would grant admitting privileges to black physicians and serve as a practical training school for black nurses.

Determined to turn her dreams into reality, Emma began saving money. In 1915, she used her savings to purchase two lots on East Eighth Street in Chattanooga, and construction soon began on a three-story building that would serve as the hospital of Emma's dreams. On July 30, 1915, dedication ceremonies were held for the new facility, named Walden Hospital. Reporting on the opening of Walden Hospital, the *Chattanooga Times* stated:

"The completion of this hospital is a work of which the colored people feel justly proud. It will be conducted by colored people, for the benefit of colored people and will enable the colored physicians to render better service to patients needing the advantages which a hospital affords than has heretofore been possible."

Dedicated exclusively to the health care of blacks, the new facility boasted thirty beds, including nine private rooms and one twelve-bed ward. Staffed by two house doctors and three nurses, Walden Hospital offered surgical, maternity, and nursery facilities.

Shortly after the opening of the hospital, seventeen physicians and surgeons from the local Mountain City Medical Society were admitting their patients to Walden Hospital. With a median monthly load of twelve patients, Walden Hospital soon became the area's primary medical facility for African Americans. In later years, Emma recalled that she had initially saved "about half enough money to pay for the building, and the hospital succeeded so well that all the notes were paid off in less than three years."

While her husband used the facility for his patients, Emma assumed sole responsibility of the hospital's management and operation. Along with her duties as hospital superintendent, she also devoted long hours to the joint medical practice that she shared with her husband, delivering hundreds of babies and performing many surgical procedures. Although a fire destroyed many of the hospital's birth records, Emma estimated that more than two thousand babies were born at Walden Hospital.

As a physician, Emma readily admitted that she favored obstetrical cases. In spite of her busy schedule, she gave birth to two more babies of her own, Thelma and Betty. Emma and her husband also added another member to their growing family with the adoption of Emma's nephew, George Wheeler.

In 1925, Emma established the Nurse Service Club of Chattanooga, an innovative, prepaid hospitalization plan. Independent of the hospital's operations, the club offered two weeks of free hospitalization and in-home nursing care after hospital discharge. During the same year, she worked with three other organizers to form the city's first Alpha Kappa Alpha chapter. Emma also operated a school for nurses, offering nursing classes and instruction with her husband's assistance for more than twenty years.

After her husband's death in 1940, Emma continued to operate Walden Hospital. During the late 1940s, a local newspaper applauded the success of the facility by writing: "The Walden Hospital has stood through the years as a beacon and ray to hope to the sick, wounded and afflicted. . . . It gives physicians of all races an opportunity to improve their medical knowledge and skill."

An inspiration to young African Americans, the enterprising hospital founder encouraged dozens of young people to pursue their educational and business dreams. To pay tribute to her remarkable efforts, Emma was honored as "Negro Mother of the Year" by the Chattanooga branch of the National Association for the Advancement of Colored People (NAACP) in 1949.

Ill health forced Emma to close the doors of Walden Hospital on June 30, 1953, but the seventy-one-year-old physician continued to accept patients at her office on the first floor of the former hospital building until her failing health would no longer allow her to do so.

On September 12, 1957, Emma died at Hubbard Hospital in Nashville, Tennessee. After funeral services at Wiley Memorial Methodist Church in Chattanooga, she was buried alongside her husband in Chattanooga's Highland Cemetery.

In Emma's honor, Chattanooga's new housing project was given the name of "Emma Wheeler Homes" by the Chattanooga Housing Authority in 1962. Tributes to the memorable physician continued when the Tennessee Historical Commission approved the placement of a state historical marker at the site of Walden Hospital in 1990.

Although the modest physician attributed the hospital's accomplishments to "the fine white and Negro doctors here who have used Walden Hospital and helped make it a success in community service," the driving force behind the success of Walden Hospital was Dr. Emma Rochelle Wheeler. Throughout its thirty-eight years of operation, Chattanooga's Walden Hospital fulfilled the health care needs of hundreds of African Americans under the direction of a remarkable Tennessee physician.

SUE SHELTON WHITE

1887–1943

Suffragist and Political Activist

A crowd of more than two hundred gathered in front of the White House on a brisk February day in 1919, drawn to the glow of dancing flames in a Grecian urn on the sidewalk. Warned that members of the National Woman's Party (NWP) intended to burn President Woodrow Wilson's words in effigy, uniformed police officers stood a few feet away, fire extinguishers in hand.

At that moment, a woman with a head of brown curls emerged from the throng, clutching a political cartoon. The cartoon featured President Wilson speaking on the topic of freedom for all in a democratic society as the head of a woman dangled from a chain on his belt.

As state chair of the NWP in Tennessee, Sue Shelton White was frustrated with President Wilson's lack of interest in the women's suffrage movement. Although he had advocated democracy at a recent European peace conference, at home President Wilson had essentially ignored his pledge to extend voting rights to American women. More than a year had passed since the House had approved the amendment, but Wilson had done nothing to help secure votes the amendment needed for passage in the Senate.

Sue Shelton White

In a desperate attempt to gain passage of the bill before the adjournment of the Sixty-fifth Congress, Sue and other NWP members were picketing the White House, maintaining "watch fires," and holding public demonstrations to gain support for their cause. Now, in protest of Wilson's unfulfilled promise to grant voting privileges to women, Sue and dozens of other NWP members were burning the president in effigy.

No sooner had Sue placed the political cartoon in the flames than the police surged forward and arrested her and thirty-eight of the NWP demonstrators. The women were hauled to jail for the night. The next morning, a judge sentenced Sue and twenty-seven of her comrades to five days in prison.

Imprisoned in damp cellblocks measuring four feet by eight feet, the NWP launched a hunger strike to protest the denial of a basic citizenship right for women in a democratic society—the right to vote.

The protests continued after their release from prison. Donning copies of their prison uniforms, the women boarded a chartered train to carry their message to the people. Touring major cities for the next twenty-six days aboard the "Prison Special," the group rallied support for their cause from South Carolina to New York.

The challenge of securing voting rights for women had just begun for Sue Shelton White. On June 4, 1919—four months after the arrests of the NWP members—the U.S. Congress finally approved the women's suffrage amendment. Over the following year, Sue rolled up her sleeves along with other members of the NWP, and worked to gain ratification of the Nineteenth Amendment from three-quarters of the forty-eight states. With much credit to Sue Shelton White, her own home state of Tennessee would become the thirty-sixth state to ratify the amendment that enabled women to vote for the first time during the presidential election of 1920.

The only Tennessee woman to be jailed for suffrage activities, Sue Shelton White rose to national prominence during a critical period in the women's suffrage movement. One of the first female court reporters in Tennessee, she became an influential voice for Southern women during the 1910s and 1920s, breaking down barriers and changing attitudes about the traditional role of females in modern American society.

Unlike many leaders of the women's suffrage movement, Sue Shelton White did not belong to an upper-class, socially prominent family with economic security. James Shelton White and Mary Calistia Swain White, Sue's parents, lived by modest means from their meager salaries as teachers.

Along with his teaching position, James served as a Methodist minister. Although Mary attended her husband's church, she refused to join the Methodist denomination due to her staunch Baptist beliefs. When a heated debate about Mary's lack of membership erupted within James's church, James responded in anger, striking the cheek of a church elder. As a result, the church expelled James from the ministry in 1879. He also lost his position at Jackson District High School, a Methodist-sponsored school in Montezuma, Tennessee.

To make a fresh start, James and Mary moved to Henderson, a rural community located a few miles from Montezuma. The couple eventually became the parents of five boys—two of whom died in early childhood—and two girls. Their sixth child, Sue Shelton White, was born in Henderson on May 25, 1887.

With James's death in 1893, Mary became responsible for caring for five children on her own. Struggling to make ends meet, Sue's mother gave piano and voice lessons, wrote and sold newspaper articles, and sometimes earned money by selling pianos and books. Mary White's situation in life greatly affected her daughter. Young Sue realized that women needed specialized training that would give them marketable skills and allow them to be independent and self-supporting. When her mother died in 1901, fourteen-year-old Sue vowed to pursue a practical education so she would not become financially dependent on others.

Following her mother's death, Sue moved into an aunt's home and enrolled in Georgia Robertson Christian College, a normal school in Henderson. As a student there Sue took classes in shorthand, bookkeeping, grammar, geography, arithmetic, and typing. She then completed another year of study at West Tennessee Business College in Dyer.

Sue landed a job as a stenographer with a manufacturing company in Jackson, Tennessee, in 1905. Ambitious and eager to advance to a better position, she displayed interest in learning more about the manufacturing business. But her eager ambitions turned to disillusioned dreams when her employer discouraged her from tackling any tasks beyond typing.

Two years later, Sue left the company and forged new ground by becoming one of the first female court reporters in Tennessee. Over the next twelve years as a court reporter—and as an independent stenographer for members of the Tennessee Supreme Court—Sue made numerous political contacts that would later become invaluable during her work for the women's suffrage movement.

At the same time, she discovered that the ambitions of working women were not highly regarded in the world of politics. Personal encounters with sexual discrimination convinced her of the need for laws that would provide equality for women. Although attorneys complimented her abilities as a court reporter, they balked when she confessed that she would like to become a lawyer. On one occasion, a Tennessee senator rejected Sue for a secretarial position—even though a judge had highly recommended her for the job—merely because she was a woman.

With her growing interest in law, politics, and women's equality, in 1912 Sue became a founding member of the Jackson league of the Tennessee Equal Suffrage Association (TESA), an affiliate of the National American Woman's Suffrage Association (NAWSA). An active member in both the local and state chapters, Sue was elected recording secretary of TESA in 1913.

By late 1916, however, Sue noticed that the suffrage campaigns of the Southern state chapters were not receiving full support from the national NAWSA group. To make matters worse, disagreement over the proposed methods for achieving women's suffrage had divided the NAWSA membership. Under the leadership of President Carrie Chapman Catt, the NAWSA had endorsed constitutional suffrage amendments on a state-by-state basis, with the ultimate goal of achieving a national constitutional amendment. But many members so strongly believed in concentrating on one national amendment to the constitution that they broke apart from the NAWSA in 1916 to form the National Women's Party (NWP).

The NWP held public demonstrations and picketed government buildings and quickly gained a reputation as the "militant" arm of the suffrage movement. In 1917, NAWSA supporters, strongly opposed to the NWP's tactics, attempted to block a NWP representative from a nine-city speaking tour of Tennessee. Civic leaders and members of the Tennessee Bar Association encouraged cities to deny all requests from the NWP for meeting permits and for space reservations.

Appalled by the state's lack of respect for the NWP, Sue leaped to the aid of NAWSA's rival organization. During the fall of 1917, she temporarily left her job as a court reporter to accompany the NWP representative, Maude Younger, on a speaking tour throughout the state. Drawing upon her contacts with state lawyers and politicians, Sue fought to preserve the NWP's schedule of speaking engagements in nine Tennessee towns.

A fellow suffragist later praised Sue for her dedication to the suffrage movement in Tennessee by writing:

> She was truly a great woman . . . [who] would do what she could for that she believed in, even when it meant adjusting her personal and business life to do it . . . [Since Sue] lived by what she earned . . . her shutting up shop to help us was a real sacrifice. Her reward, as always, was the knowledge she had done right.

But in early 1918, Sue's activities were not lauded with such lavish praise. As the recording secretary of a state organization, Sue must have been amazed when her activities attracted the attention of Carrie Chapman Catt, NAWSA president and the country's most visible and influential suffrage leader. In a letter to Kate Werner, president of the TESA, Carrie complained about Sue's involvement with the rival organization, concerned that Sue might reveal some of the NAWSA's operating plans to the NWP.

In defense of her work for the NWP, Sue responded with a letter to the national president. Her initial sympathy for the harassed NWP workers, she explained, developed into serious interest in the NWP only after she learned that the NAWSA was cutting back on support for state campaigns in the South. In a letter to Carrie on April 27, 1918, she wrote:

> I am always willing to "face the music" and answer for my own acts with as little embarrassment to my friends as possible. . . . After it developed that the southern states could not expect any assistance from the National for the Federal Amendment work, I became a great deal more interested in the work of the Woman's Party in the South.

. . . I place my interest in the suffrage cause above my interest in any one suffrage organization, [but] I am more inclined than I would have otherwise been to lend "co-operation" to the National Woman's Party, since it is working in the southern states and the National is not.

In response, Carrie denied that the national NAWSA group was abandoning the Tennessee suffragists. She also demanded that Sue choose between the NAWSA and NWP. "This is the period," she wrote, "in which women everywhere must take a big view and try to consider all the data before making up their minds. . . . Get the data and think the matter out to a conclusion and then take your stand fair and square, one side or the other."

Torn between loyalty to the NAWSA and her distaste for their treatment of the NWP membership, Sue expressed her concerns in a second letter to Carrie on May 9, 1918:

What shall be my own fate, I do not know. I have been the official "goat" of Tennessee suffragedom ever since I came into the work. I may be thrown by main strength and awkwardness into the bosom of the National Woman's Party. There I shall find a welcome, I am sure, but it . . . may mean the greatest sacrifice I could make.

The following month, after breaking ties with the NAWSA and TESA, Sue was named chair of the NWP in Tennessee. The "sacrifice" that she had hoped to avoid became reality in February 1919 when Sue was arrested and thrown in jail for burning President Wilson's words in effigy at a demonstration in front of the White House.

"I found that almost unaware I had committed myself. I became a suffragist, an active one, finally a militant one," Sue wrote in an anonymous, autobiographical article, "Mother's Daughter," published by *The Nation* magazine in 1926.

Fully committed to the NWP, Sue was named editor of the group's national newspaper, the *Suffragist*, in 1919. And she assumed more responsibilities in the battle for women's suffrage when the fight escalated into a raging war in 1920.

By the late spring of 1920, thirty-five states had ratified the suffrage amendment. To gain access to the ballot boxes during the presidential election of 1920, suffragists needed the approval of only one more state to complete the ratification by three-fourths of the forty-eight states, the number required for a constitutional amendment.

Then, in mid-June, progress came to a dead halt. Connecticut, Vermont, and Florida refused to call their legislatures into session to consider ratification. Tensions mounted as North Carolina legislators defeated the amendment, and the focus shifted to Tennessee. Could the Volunteer State help the suffrage cause?

As Tennessee chair of the NWP, Sue assumed the responsibility of requesting a special session of the Tennessee legislature. Backed by the state attorney general, Sue penned the request in a letter to Governor Albert H. Roberts on June 19, 1920.

To her delight and that of her fellow suffragists, the Tennessee governor granted the request. On August 9, the state legislature convened in special session. The decision of whether women would vote in the November election now rested with Tennessee.

Suffragists flocked to Nashville for the event. Throughout three weeks of heated political debate, women from across the nation crowded into local hotels and vied for gallery seats on the House floor. One observer noted, "The Battle of Nashville in 1864 was a five o'clock tea in comparison with this one."

A hospitality suite on the eighth floor of the Hermitage Hotel, sponsored by anti-suffrage liquor lobbyists, dispensed Tennessee-brewed Jack Daniel's whiskey around the clock during the special legislative session. Lingering in the corridor outside the "Jack Daniels Suite," Sue and a fellow suffragist hoped to overhear snippets of news from the anti-suffragists. Their eavesdropping antics made the headlines in the *Chattanooga Times*. In a front-page article, "Two Women Spies Caught in Hotel," the newspaper reported that "Two wily, militant suffragists undertook to snatch information from the anti-suffrage forces on the eighth floor of the Hermitage." The suffragists left the area, the article explained, only after the hotel proprietor escorted them to a waiting elevator and closed the door.

But victory was close at hand. On Friday, August 13, 1920, the Tennessee senate passed the resolution of ratification. And on the following Wednesday, August 18, the state house passed the resolution with a majority of a single vote, making Tennessee the pivotal state needed to complete ratification of the national "Susan B. Anthony Amendment." On Tuesday, August 26, the Nineteenth Amendment to the U.S. Constitution took effect, proclaiming that the right of citizens "to vote shall not be denied or abridged by the United States or by any State on account of sex."

After the 1920 suffrage victory, Sue set her sights on other, more personal dreams. Moving to Washington, D.C., she worked as a secretary to Tennessee Senator Kenneth McKellar and pursued her goal of becoming a lawyer by taking legal courses at night. In 1923, she received a law degree from Washington College of Law and was admitted to the bar.

Still active in the NWP, she immediately put her law degree to work for the cause of women's rights, studying discriminatory provisions in state legal codes and assisting in the development of a bill that would prohibit discrimination against women. The bill that Sue helped to write—the original version of the Equal Rights Amendment—was introduced in Congress in 1923.

In 1926, Sue returned to Tennessee, opened a law practice in

Jackson, and distinguished herself as the city's first female attorney. Four years later, she returned to the nation's capitol to serve as executive assistant to the vice chairman of the Democratic National Committee and executive secretary of the women's division of the Democratic party.

During the Roosevelt administration, Sue remained active in government and politics. After serving as assistant to the chairman of the Consumers Advisory Board of the National Recovery Administration, she became the first attorney for the Social Security Board in 1936. Two years later, she was named as the principal attorney and assistant to the general counsel of the Federal Security Agency. And she continued her work for women's rights until her death from cancer on May 6, 1943.

Perhaps Sue best defined her philosophy toward women's rights during a 1926 speech to the Jackson Business & Professional Women's Club:

> We must remember the past, hold fast to the present, and build for the future. If you stand in our accepted place today, it is because some woman had to fight yesterday. We should be ashamed to stand on ground won by women in the past without making an effort to honor them by winning a higher and wider field for the future. It is a debt we owe.

BESSIE SMITH

1894–1937

Empress of the Blues

*B*risk winds whipped through the woman's threadbare coat as she stood in front of New York's Columbia Recording Studio. She shivered, acutely aware the frigid air was not the cause of the chills coursing through her. On that blustery winter morning in 1923, Bessie Smith was trembling from a severe case of jittery nerves.

Within a few moments, she would be auditioning for Frank Walker, a music executive in charge of recording race material for Columbia. Years ago, Frank had heard her sing at a little dive in Selma, Alabama, and now that he was responsible for acquiring new talent at Columbia, he'd remembered her performance and requested that she audition for him.

Bessie hesitantly entered the building with her accompanist, Clarence, and tried to push aside her memories of unsuccessful auditions with other recording companies in recent years. Most studio executives contended her voice was either too rough, too raw, or too unsophisticated for their labels. The owner of one company, Thomas Edison, claimed her voice was "no good." And her audition at Black Swan Records had ended in dismal failure when she'd abruptly stopped singing to say, "Hold on! Let me spit."

Bessie Smith

Worse yet, Bessie knew the odds of a black woman being accepted by any recording company were not favorable. Although several black females had recorded songs in recent years, neither their music nor their voices had been widely accepted. Still, fate was giving Bessie Smith one more chance to become a famous singer.

Determined to momentarily set aside her doubts and fears, she stepped into Columbia's recording studio and inhaled a deep, steadying breath. Accompanied by Clarence on the piano, she began to sing. As her rich, deep voice filled the studio, Frank Walker immediately realized that Bessie Smith's musical talents were as big and powerful as the woman herself. Nearly six feet tall with extremely dark skin, Bessie packed about two hundred pounds of weight behind a magnificent, mesmerizing voice.

When the audition was over, Bessie signed a recording contract with Columbia. Years later, Frank recalled the day of Bessie's audition. "The girl . . . looked like anything but a singer. She looked about seventeen—tall and fat and scared to death—just awful! But all of this you forgot when you heard her sing."

Bessie recorded her first song, "Down-Hearted Blues," for Columbia on February 17, 1923. Other singers had previously recorded the tune, but Bessie's version sold 780,000 copies, surpassing the combined sales of the work of all other female blues singers.

Between February and June 1923, Bessie recorded eighteen songs for Columbia, accompanied only by piano on most of the recordings. Columbia, which had been teetering on the brink of bankruptcy, experienced a sharp jump in record sales. Within a short time, fans had bought two million of Bessie's records—more than any other Columbia artist had ever sold. Soon the recording company was billing her as "The Empress of the Blues."

During the 1920s Bessie Smith became one of the most famous black women of the era. Along the way, she also became a legend in American music. According to jazz historian Rosetta Reitz:

Bessie Smith is undoubtedly the most important woman in the history of American music. She was the first to change a folk expression into an indigenous art form by successfully blending African and Western modes of music. The blues-jazz she sang is the most significant base of America's contribution to world culture: blues and jazz.

The only official record of Bessie Smith's birth on April 15, 1894, is her claim to that date on a 1920 marriage license. Small Southern towns like Chattanooga, Tennessee, Bessie's birthplace, rarely maintained accurate birth records of blacks before the twentieth century.

Poverty encompassed Bessie's early years. The second of seven children, young Bessie grew up in a one-room shanty. Her father William, a part-time Baptist minister, died during her childhood. To help with household expenses, Bessie sang on the streets of Chattanooga, collecting nickels and dimes from appreciative street audiences.

By the age of nine, Bessie had earned the grand sum of eight dollars for her first professional singing engagement on stage at a local theater. To celebrate her good fortune she promptly purchased a pair of roller skates with her earnings. Unfortunately, the celebration ended when her mother disciplined her with a sound beating for squandering the money.

Laura Smith, Bessie's mother, died soon after this incident, leaving Bessie and her siblings on their own. Opportunities for young, black girls in the South at the time were limited to tending children, cleaning houses, or washing clothes for meager wages. Bessie found a different way to make money. Dropping out of school, she returned to the street corners and sang for small change. Her brother Andrew accompanied her on guitar.

Another brother, Clarence, who also wanted to perform, joined a traveling minstrel show as a dancer-comedian. Dozens of road companies traveled from town to town during the early years of the twentieth century, entertaining black audiences in tent shows, theaters, carnivals, and circuses. Undoubtedly, Clarence's entry into show business as a member of the Moses Stokes Traveling Show impressed his sister. In 1912, Bessie joined her brother on the road as a singer in the Rabbit Foot Minstrels, part of the Moses Stokes troupe. Years later, rumors circulated that Gertrude "Ma" Rainey, star of the Rabbit Foot Minstrels, kidnapped Bessie after hearing her magnificent voice and forced her to join the troupe. More reliable sources, however, contend that Clarence arranged a successful audition for Bessie with Moses Stokes's show.

Unable to resist other opportunities for singing, Bessie soon obtained a regular "gig" at Atlanta's 81 Theater for ten dollars a week. She spent the remainder of the 1910s performing on the black vaudeville circuit with road companies such as Pete Werley's Florida Cotton Blossoms. For more than five years, she was featured in traveling road shows through the Theatre Owners Booking Association (TOBA), working in tents, carnivals, and honky-tonks throughout the Southeast.

In spite of her busy schedule, Bessie found time for romance. She met and married Earl Love in 1920. The marriage, however, ended with Earl's death the following year.

Like many other African Americans of the day, Bessie believed the North held more opportunities for jobs and money than her native South. During the early 1920s, Bessie packed her bags and headed for the East Coast, performing in major cities. She eventually settled in Philadelphia and married former Philadelphia policeman Jack Gee in 1923.

With the overwhelming success of the 1923 release of "Down-Hearted Blues," the public demanded more personal appearances by

Bessie Smith. Her deep, expressive voice appealed to people. Unlike other singers, Bessie did not need a megaphone to be heard in large theaters. Some fans claimed they could even hear her powerful voice from the street when she was performing on a stage inside the theater. Fans also insisted her overwhelming stage presence was unforgettable. On stage, she wore outlandish hats, fanciful turbans, and dresses trimmed with beaded satin, heavy fringes, and ostrich feathers.

No other singer possessed a voice like Bessie Smith's. As she sang of suffering, joy, betrayal, and courage, her voice slid up, down, and around notes with remarkable intensity and power. While singing, she took breaths and carried over her voice in unexpected places. Her enunciation was clear and precise; her style was all her own. "Once she started to sing, nobody told her what to do. Nobody interfered," Frank Walker later explained.

Acoustical recordings emphasized the deep richness of Bessie's voice. Since microphones were not available in the 1920s, Bessie and other singers of the day made acoustical recordings by singing into the large mouth of a huge horn. Voice vibrations activated the cutting tool, or stylus, at the small end of the horn. The stylus cut grooves into a thick, waxy disc that became the master record. Machines in record factories produced copies from this master record, which were then shipped to stores.

Bessie's talents impressed not only record fans but fellow musicians. During a 1925 recording session of nine songs, including the classics "St. Louis Blues" and "Careless Love," Bessie was accompanied by Fletcher Henderson's orchestra. One musician who had recently joined the orchestra was a young man by the name of Louis Armstrong. During an interview in the 1940s, Armstrong recalled Bessie's abilities: "Bessie used to thrill me at all times. It's the way she could phrase a note in her blues, a certain something in her voice that no other singer could get. . . . She really had music in her soul and felt everything she did."

Columbia soon billed Bessie as the "greatest and highest sala-ried race star in the world." Although she initially received a flat fee of $125 per side for her records, Columbia eventually increased the payments to $200. Between earnings from radio shows, recordings, and personal appearances, Bessie's income soared. From 1924 to 1927, the blues singer earned as much as two thousand dollars per week.

She spent the money as fast as she made it. She moved her brothers and sisters to Philadelphia, bought a farm in New Jersey, and purchased a luxurious railroad car for traveling the tent show circuit. Her extravagant purchases became a hot topic among her fans.

In spite of her success, Bessie led a tumultuous life. Bold and aggressive, she garnered the reputation of being tough on other en-tertainers who might threaten her success. Drinking binges fueled her hot temper. On occasion, she actually hit people who annoyed her and instigated backstage brawls.

Bessie's dependence on alcohol had increased dramatically by the end of the 1920s. Her heavy drinking often led to missed per-formances or cancellations at theaters and night clubs. Old friends began to refuse to work with her. "She was full of life, but she had to have that booze." Gwendolyn Bailey, Bessie's great-niece, revealed to a newspaper reporter in 1987. Gwendolyn also claimed that Bessie's favorite remedy to sober up was to eat a can of pink salmon drenched in hot sauce.

While Bessie's drinking binges grew more frequent, musical tastes were changing. Although she starred in her first and only film, *St. Louis Blues*, in 1929, the public already had begun to abandon her gaudy, sometimes crude style in favor of more sophisticated blues singing. As a result, her earnings dipped dramatically. Hoping to win back her fans, Bessie replaced her "old-time blues" with smoother, more sophisticated songs. Her manager, Frank Walker, disagreed with the change, so Bessie immediately appointed her husband as her new manager.

But the days of big earnings and lavish spending sprees were at an end. Bessie's 1929 recording, "Nobody Knows You When You're Down and Out," appropriately reflected the turmoil in her own life. The classic blues era was over—along with Bessie's career and means of income. Even her marriage fell apart when her husband took off with Gertrude Saunders, another entertainer.

The financial plight of the country only made matters worse. Bessie struggled to survive during the Depression. She modified her flamboyant lifestyle, exchanging her gaudy costumes for simple, elegant gowns. She adopted a sleek, sophisticated hairstyle by brushing her hair back from her face. Still, people without jobs or money couldn't buy records or pay to see their favorite singers. Due to declining sales, Columbia Records dropped Bessie from their label in 1931. Two years later, she recorded several songs for Okeh Records, receiving only thirty-seven dollars per side.

But Bessie continued to persevere. She received rave reviews from fans and critics when she replaced rising star Billie Holliday for a six-week engagement at a mid-town Manhattan club in 1935. This, coupled with the arrival of a new man in her life, Richard Morgan, uncle of jazz musician Lionel Hampton, apparently rallied her spirits.

Bessie hit the road again in 1937 with her own show: the Bessie Smith Revue. Accompanied by Richard, she traveled to performances throughout the South in an old Packard. Sadly, the tour ended in tragedy along a highway between Memphis, Tennessee, and Clarksdale, Mississippi. With Richard at the wheel, the Packard crashed into a parked truck on the side of the road. The impact hurled Bessie from the car, nearly severing her right arm. She died from her injuries on September 26, 1937, in a Clarksdale hospital.

Stories soon spread that Bessie had been refused admittance to a nearby white hospital and bled to death from her injuries on the side of the road. But in a 1987 newspaper interview, Dr. Hugh Smith, who had passed by the scene and stopped to attend to Bessie, confirmed that she had been transported directly to the local hospital for blacks. The physician insisted that her injuries had been too extensive for survival.

More than seven thousand people attended Bessie's funeral on October 4, 1937, in Philadelphia, Pennsylvania. Tragically, the woman whose music had touched so many lives throughout the 1920s was laid to rest in an unmarked grave, apparently due to Bessie's lack of financial resources at the time of her death.

But her music lived on. In 1970, Columbia reissued more than 160 of Bessie's Columbia recordings on five double albums. The albums received two Grammy awards, and *Billboard* magazine honored Bessie with the "Trendsetter of the Year Award."

The publicity generated from the awards prompted a Philadelphia housewife to write a letter to the local newspaper about Bessie's unmarked grave. As a result, two individuals contributed funds to purchase a marker for Bessie's grave—rock singer Janis Joplin, whose own music had been greatly influenced by Bessie Smith; and Juanita Green, a black woman who had once cleaned Bessie's house and later became president of the North Philadelphia chapter of the National Association for the Advancement of Colored People (NAACP). The grave marker at Mount Lawn Cemetery in Sharon Hills, Philadelphia reads:

The Greatest Blues Singer in the World
Will Never Stop Singing
Bessie Smith
1894–1937
Unlike hundreds of singers whose music has long been forgotten, many of Bessie's recordings have been available continuously

since their initial release. Bessie and her unique style significantly influenced the careers of many singing artists, ranging from gospel singer Mahalia Jackson to jazz great Billie Holliday. Alberta Hunter, blues singer, insisted:

> Bessie Smith was the greatest of them all. There never was one like her and there'll never be one like her again. Even though she was raucous and loud, she had a sort of tear—no, not a tear, but there was misery in what she did. It was as though there was something she had to get out, something she just had to bring to the fore.

Today, the works of Bessie Smith are considered blues masterpieces. Gunther Schuller, author of *Early Jazz* and the former president of the New England Conservatory of Music, claimed:

> More than any other singer she set the blues tradition in terms of style and quality. She not only gave a special musical aura to this tradition, but her own singing and the accompaniments of the many great jazz artists who assisted her in her recordings placed it firmly in the broader jazz tradition.

GRACE MOORE

1898–1947

The Tennessee Nightingale

*G*race Moore entered her New York apartment, returning from her second audition with the Metropolitan Opera. Dismayed and stunned by the outcome of the audition, the lovely soprano from Tennessee sank into the nearest chair and reached for the phone. Within a few moments, she was talking with Otto Kahn, a wealthy banker who served as the Metropolitan Opera's president and chairman. Otto had been kind enough to arrange the audition for Grace. He listened intently as she related the events of her second attempt to join the nation's most esteemed opera company.

The criticism of the jurors had been brutal, she recalled. They had insisted she should stop trying for something beyond her abilities. They had even claimed her voice had lost color, resonance, and pitch since her previous audition.

Grace refused to be defeated by the stinging remarks from the elite panel of jurors. After all, critics had raved about her voice when she'd appeared in Irving Berlin's 1923 *Music Box Revue*. Resolving to prove that the jury had been wrong in their assessment, Grace vowed she would be accepted by the Met within the next two years. Convinced she possessed the talents and skills to become a leading

Grace Moore

primadonna, she ended the phone conversation with the chairman by wagering one hundred dollars on her predicted success.

True to her vow, Grace Moore obtained a third audition with the Met in 1927 and promptly received a contract for the upcoming season. On February 7, 1928, she made her debut, singing the role of Mimi in Puccini's *La Boheme*. Her sensational performance defied the harsh judgement of earlier critics, garnered twenty-five curtain calls, and prompted one reviewer to write:

> It is not just a lovely voice but an organ with personality.
> . . . It is exquisitely colored and vibrant, with the deep
> quality of a good Stradivarius. Musical comedy is a strange
> apprenticeship for musicianship, but Miss Moore uses
> her lovely organ with the innate sensibility of a natural
> musician. Her phrasing . . . was a model of refinement. .
> . . She imbued her muse with the proper colors of the
> sentiments they described without the smallest sacrifice
> of tonal balance and musical line.

With her 1928 debut at the Metropolitan Opera, Grace Moore launched a musical career that would thrill appreciative fans for nearly two decades. During the 1930s and 1940s, the soprano brought grace and glamour to the world of opera, becoming the toast of American and European audiences. At the same time, her popular movies introduced millions to the opera. As the first actress to sing operatic arias on film, Grace defied cultural restrictions, achieving stardom on both the big screen and the opera stage. Along the way, Grace Moore became known throughout the world as a nightingale of song.

When Mary Willie Grace Moore was born on December 6, 1898, little did her parents realize that their daughter would grow up to become an internationally acclaimed soprano. To Tessie and

Richard Moore, the rest of the world seemed very distant and remote from their isolated existence in the foothills of Tennessee's Great Smoky Mountains. Life in Slabtown, a lumber village in Cocke County, consisted primarily of visits with neighboring relatives, annual harvest celebrations, and weekly church services.

The oldest of eight children—three of whom died during childhood—Grace moved from Slabtown with her family during her early years. The Moores lived in Knoxville for a brief time, then settled in Jellico, a small coal-mining town in the heart of the Cumberland Mountains near the border between Tennessee and Kentucky. Her father established a wholesale dry goods business in Jellico that eventually prospered.

Devoted Baptists, the Moores were active members of the First Baptist Church of Jellico. Grace was introduced to music at an early age through her family's church participation. She sang her first solo, "Rock of Ages," as a member of the children's choir.

But the rigid moral codes of the Baptist faith—and her father's strict rules of personal conduct—contrasted sharply with Grace's fascination with the arts and her strong-willed personality. At eighteen, she was condemned for dancing at a party and forced to confess her sins before the church congregation. Humiliated, Grace promptly devised a plan to leave Jellico. Furthering her education seemed like the most logical avenue of escape from the small town.

In September 1916, Grace enrolled as a student at Ward-Belmont School for Girls in Nashville. Exposed to life outside her narrow world for the first time, the young woman became acutely aware of her Tennessee accent. Grace concentrated on her singing lessons with such intensity that she ignored other class assignments. By the end of the first term, she was expelled from school for poor grades.

Undaunted, Grace set her sights higher. A few months after leaving Nashville, she informed her father that she had been corresponding with the Wilson-Greene School of Music in Washington, D.C. The school had already accepted her as a student, she explained. Could she leave for the nation's capitol with his blessings?

Although Richard Moore strongly disapproved of a musical career for his daughter, he did not have the heart to refuse her request to continue her education. Within a few months, Grace was studying French, dramatic art, sight-reading, and piano at Wilson-Greene. She eventually earned ten dollars per week, her first salary, for singing in the choir of Calvary Baptist Church in Washington, D.C.

At the same time, Grace's dreams for the future came into sharper focus. As a student at the music school, Grace took advantage of opportunities to attend musical concerts and meet performing artists in Washington. After hearing and meeting Mary Garden, the internationally famous prima donna and leading soprano of the Chicago Civic Opera Company, Grace knew precisely what she wanted to achieve in life. She wanted to become a dynamic opera prima donna—another Mary Garden.

She diligently worked to improve her musical skills, then auditioned and received a role in the school's annual concert. On February 20, 1919, Grace Moore made her debut at the National Theater with Giovanni Martinelli, one of the leading tenors of the Metropolitan Opera. One Washington critic described her as "a young lyric soprano from Tennessee who showed promise." The favorable review gave Grace all the encouragement she needed to head for New York and pursue a stage career. Only after arriving in the city did she inform her family of her whereabouts. Outraged by his daughter's impulsive behavior, Richard Moore promptly traveled to New York and insisted she return home with him.

But Grace had other ideas. She refused to return to Jellico, and her father went home without her. Soon she was working at a night club in Greenwich Village, singing for supper and seventy-five dollars a week. She also relentlessly auditioned for singing roles and won parts in several stage shows. "First You Wiggle—Then You Waggle," her sole song in the musical comedy, *Suite Sixteen*, was one of her earliest triumphs. An audition with Jerome Kern resulted in a small part in another show, *Hitchy Koo*. By 1921, even her father could no longer deny that Grace Moore possessed a remarkable voice. After witnessing one of her performances in Cincinnati, Richard Moore finally gave his approval to Grace's pursuit of a musical career.

Though pleased with her success in musical comedy, Grace continued to dream of becoming an acclaimed opera star. After a second encounter with Mary Garden, Grace became convinced that she must study and perform abroad if she hoped to achieve her goal of becoming a Met prima donna.

Keeping her sights on a career in opera, Grace sailed for Europe. But a few weeks after arriving in Paris, she accepted a tempting offer that temporarily changed the direction of her career. When composer Irving Berlin offered her a leading role in the 1923 edition of *Music Box Revue* and an overwhelming salary, Grace could not refuse the generous contract. Bidding *adieu* to Paris, she immediately returned to New York for rehearsals.

Music Box Revue opened on September 22, 1923. The show was an instant hit. Grace's photo appeared on the front page of the *New York Times*, and friends and fans toasted her performance with streams of telegrams, notes, and flowers. Most importantly, the moment marked Grace Moore as a rising musical star. Author Rowena Raffe noted: "As the sparkling notes poured from her throat, a kind of magic took place. Grace fell in love with the audience and they with her. She proved she possessed not only a beautiful voice, but that rare mysterious something called 'star quality.'"

Although Grace relished the acclaim and huge salary from her work on the stage, the dream of performing with the Met continued to haunt her. Determined to achieve her goal, she auditioned for the Met in 1924. The jury concluded she was not yet ready for the demands of the Metropolitan Opera but politely asked her to return for another audition in one year. Grace's second attempt at winning the judges' hearts, however, resulted in the stinging critique that prompted her to proclaim she would win a different verdict from the jury within the next two years.

With renewed determination, Grace bid farewell to Broadway's musical comedy and financial security, and sailed for Europe in 1925. Living in Mary Garden's apartment in Monte Carlo, she concentrated on her musical studies with Garden's favorite accompanist and operatic coach, Richard Barthelemy. Two years later, Otto arranged a third audition for her with the Met in Milan, Italy. This time, Grace won a contract for the upcoming season at a salary of seventy-five dollars per week.

Members of the press and more than one hundred people from Tennessee—including the Moore family, now fully in favor of Grace's singing career—traveled by special train to New York for Grace's 1928 debut. Nervous with stage fright, Grace fumbled through the first act but quickly regained her composure to enjoy twenty-five curtain calls and magnificent reviews.

Grace knew she must improve her stage presence and musicianship if she intended to thrill audiences at sold-out performances. She returned to Europe, performing in small opera houses to gain more experience. She eventually sang in the Paris Opera-Comique, mesmerizing the audience with her performance.

With each passing month, her earnings steadily increased. A lover of the finer things in life, Grace splurged on a limousine, chauffeur, and French maid. She also indulged in her passions for fine art, sparkling jewels, and a fabulous wardrobe. But by the time Grace returned to New York, financial woes were plaguing the country from the 1929 stock market crash. The Met had fallen on hard times, and "talking pictures" were catching the public's fancy. Never one to resist the opportunity to scale new heights, Grace eagerly accepted an invitation for a screen test with Metro-Goldwyn-Mayer Studios. The result was a three-year contract with MGM.

In her first movie, *A Lady's Morals*, Grace played Jenny Lind, the "Swedish Nightingale." Although the 1931 picture included the first complete operatic scenes ever filmed, audiences were not impressed. After a second box-office flop, *New Moon*, Grace was dropped from MGM's roster of stars.

Nursing her wounds, Grace headed for Europe once again. A shipboard romance with Spanish actor Valentin Parera lifted her spirits, and Grace fell madly in love with the handsome actor. In July 1931, Grace and Val were married at Cannes City Hall in France.

The Depression forced Grace to seek other avenues for her music. During 1933, she sang as a guest artist on several radio shows and performed numerous concerts throughout the country. And she discovered the movie industry was still interested in her talents, in spite of the failure of her earlier films.

After a concert at the Hollywood Bowl, Grace met Harry Cohn, president and chief stockholder of a small company known as Columbia Pictures. Although Grace had never heard of Cohn or Columbia, she learned the company was ready to distribute its first film, *It Happened One Night*, starring Claudette Colbert and Clark Gable. When Cohn promised to deliver a script that would allow her to sing operatic arias on film once again, Grace accepted the contract offer. For the next few months, she focused her attention on filming the picture *One Night of Love*.

The movie was a sensational hit with both critics and audiences. After a gala premiere at Radio City Music Hall in 1934, critics hailed the film as a four-star hit and one of the ten best of all time. The press claimed Grace Moore was the most glamorous and sophisticated American woman in the world. As fans flocked to see the movie, Grace ranked as the second most popular box-office star of the year. And at the 1934 Academy Awards, Victor Schertzinger received an Oscar for composing the movie's title song, *One Night of Love*, which Grace sang in the film.

Overnight, it seemed, the movie created instant popularity for Grace. In her autobiography, she reflected on the success of the film:

> Quite objectively, I can look back on the movie, *One Night of Love*, filmed in 1934, and see what it meant in terms of music. It took grand opera to the ends of the world and brought a new public into the opera houses to rejuvenate and refresh what had become a baronial subscription art. . . . "It took the high-hat off opera," editorialized the *Daily News* in New York. . . . Here was not only personal triumph. It meant more than that to me. It meant a new lease on life for the music I loved. . . .

Continuing to broaden her appeal, Grace again performed on radio shows. During weekly, half-hour radio broadcasts in the mid-1930s, she became one of the first performers to talk informally between songs about her selections and her career.

In 1934, the Society of Arts and Sciences unanimously awarded her its National Service Fellowship Medal. The first representative of the film world to receive the award, Grace joined the ranks of other distinguished recipients such as Thomas A. Edison and John Philip Sousa. In the fifty-two years of the Society's existence, only one other woman out of sixteen recipients had received the honor.

Grace's musical versatility and universal appeal landed her starring roles in numerous movies while continuing to thrill concert audiences. Between 1934 and 1937, she crisscrossed the Atlantic each year to meet her obligations to both live audiences and film production studios. In great demand, she sang at command performances for European royalty and eventually received fourteen medals from heads of state. Her distinguished audiences included King Gustav of Sweden, Queen Mary of England, and the Duke of Windsor and his bride, Wallis Warfield Simpson.

From common man to European royalty, everyone loved Grace Moore. And everyone knew who she was, as she recalled in her autobiography: "I learned through the run of *One Night of Love* that fame in the usual sense has nothing to do with the universal familiarity you gain through the screen. Hollywood made my face, my voice, my name completely recognizable here, in Europe, throughout the world."

The prima donna was not always the picture of perfection, however. Grace openly admitted that she had inherited her mother's tendency to sulk and exaggerate when life was not going her way. Worse yet, she often resorted to temper tantrums, especially when stressed beyond her limits.

During the production of a movie in 1937, Grace's character flaws became evident when a producer tried to tell her how to sing. Disgusted with the man's audacity, she walked off the set. Weary of contending with the demands of the film industry, Grace bought out her contract—refusing to make three additional movies—and bid farewell to Hollywood.

While Grace was winning the hearts of fans across the globe during the 1930s, her father purchased a Chattanooga department store and relocated the family to the small city on the Tennessee–Georgia border. After spending a delightful Thanksgiving in Chattanooga with her family, Grace and Val settled in Connecticut, purchasing a historic saltbox home. Their new residence became known as "Far Away Meadows Farm."

Determined to concentrate solely on her operatic career, Grace filmed the popular opera *Louise* in the Paramount studios near Paris in 1938. The threat of war looming over Europe, however, sent her scurrying back to the United States, where she discovered herself in even greater demand.

Along with singing to sold-out audiences for fabulous fees, Grace appeared on many lists as one of ten best dressed women in America. Even the federal government recognized Grace's influence throughout the world. In 1941, the U.S. Department of State asked Grace to become the first American artist to make a goodwill singing tour. One of the pioneers of the State Department's Cultural Exchange Program, Grace received an enthusiastic reception in Mexico as "U.S. Good-Will Singing Ambassadress." Impressed with the results of her Mexican performance, the state department then scheduled a South American tour featuring Grace as "North American Good-Will Ambassadress."

With the advent of World War II, Grace served as a USO volunteer long before entertainers were officially scheduled to perform for troops. Paying her own travel expenses from camp to camp, she offered troops free admission to her concerts. During the winter and spring of 1943, Grace performed eighty-three concerts and many radio broadcasts for the U.S. Treasury Department's war bond drive.

At the close of the war, Grace continued touring and singing to the liberated peoples of Europe. But a successful Copenhagen concert in early 1947 marked the end of Grace Moore's sensational career. On January 26, 1947, Grace departed from Copenhagen on a twin-engine plane headed to Stockholm. Among the plane's twenty-two occupants were six crew members and sixteen passengers, including Prince Gustav Adolph of Sweden, next in line for the Swedish throne. Grace was the only American on board.

After takeoff, the plane stalled, shuddered, and nose-dived to the ground. The crew and passengers—including the Tennessee nightingale—died instantly. An investigation later revealed that human error had been the cause of the crash. A clamp for locking the aircraft into position while on the ground had not been removed before takeoff.

The world mourned the loss of the magnificent songstress. Memorial services were held across the globe from Connecticut to Copenhagen. At Grace's funeral, more than two thousand mourners crowded into the First Baptist Church in Chattanooga and another four thousand stood outside the sanctuary, listening to the broadcast services. Grace Moore was laid to rest at Forest Hills Cemetery in Chattanooga.

In his eloquent eulogy of Grace Moore, Reverend John A. Huff, minister of First Baptist Church in Chattanooga, expressed the sentiments of thousands of grieving fans across the globe:

> Her golden voice has been heard by thousands in concert halls all over the world and by millions over the radio. Wherever she has been heard, from the palace of kings to the humble cottage beside the road, human hearts have been blessed by her joyous music.

ℬIBLIOGRAPHY

GENERAL REFERENCES

Dykeman, Wilma. *Tennessee Woman, An Infinite Variety.* Newport, TN: Wakestone Books, 1993.

"Women in Tennessee History: An Online Bibliography & Research Guide." Todd Library, Middle Tennessee State University. Online, 1998. Available http://www.mtsu.edu/~kmiddlet/history/womtnbib.html. Accessed April 20, 1999.

NANCY WARD

Alderman, Pat. *Nancy Ward, Cherokee Chieftainess.* Johnson City, TN: The Overmountain Press, 1990.

Cornwell, Ilene J. "Nancy Ward," in *Heroes of Tennessee,* ed. by Billy M. Jones. Memphis, TN: Memphis State University Press, 1979.

Felton, Harold W. *Nancy Ward, Cherokee.* New York: Dodd, Mead, and Company, 1975.

McKissack, Patricia and Fredrick McKissack. *Tennessee Trailblazers.* Brentwood, TN: March Media, 1993.

"Nancy Ward," in *UXL Biographies.* Detroit, MI: Gale Research, Inc., 1996. Online, Women's History Resource Center 1999. Available http://www.gale.com/gale/cwh/cwhset.html. Accessed January 15, 1999.

RACHEL DONELSON JACKSON

Caroli, Betty Boyd. "Young Substitutes for First Ladies (1829–1869)," in *First Ladies.* New York and Oxford: Oxford University Press, 1987.

Govan, Christine. *Rachel Jackson: Tennessee Girl.* Indianapolis and New York: The Bobbs–Merrill Company, Inc., 1955, reprinted 1962.

Minnigerode, Meade. *Some American Ladies, Seven Informal Biographies.* Freeport, NY: Books for Libraries Press, 1926, reprinted 1969.

Vance, Marguerite. *The Jacksons of Tennessee.* New York: E.P. Dutton & Company, Inc., 1953.

SARAH CHILDRESS POLK

Bergeron, Paul H. "All in the Family: President Polk in the White House," *Tennessee Historical Quarterly*, Vol. 46, Spring 1987.

Caroli, Betty Boyd. "Three Exceptions: Sarah Childress Polk, Mary Todd Lincoln, and Julia Dent Grant," in *First Ladies.* New York and Oxford: Oxford University Press, 1987.

Claxton, Jimmie Lou Sparkman. *88 Years with Sarah Polk.* New York: Vantage Press, 1972.

Wallace, Sarah Agnes, ed. "Letters of Mrs. James K. Polk to Her Husband," *Tennessee Historical Quarterly*, Vol. 11, 1952.

ELIZA MCCARDLE JOHNSON

Caroli, Betty Boyd. "Young Substitutes for First Ladies (1829–1869)," in *First Ladies.* New York and Oxford: Oxford University Press, 1987.

Galletta, Jan. "Clinton's Woes Prompt New Interest in Johnson," *Chattanooga Times and Free Press*, February 7, 1999.

Trefousse, Hans L. *Andrew Johnson: A Biography.* New York: W.W. Norton & Company, 1989.

ELIZABETH MCGAVOCK HARDING

Jones, Katherine M., ed. *Heroines of Dixie: Spring of High Hopes.* St. Simons Island, GA: Mockingbird Books, 1986. Originally published by The Bobbs–Merrill Company, 1955.

Wills, Ridley, II. *The History of Belle Meade: Mansion, Plantation, and Stud.* Nashville, TN: Vanderbilt University Press, 1991.

———. "Letters from Nashville, 1862, I. A Portrait of Belle Meade," *Tennessee Historical Quarterly*, Vol. 33, 1974.

ELIZABETH MERIWETHER GILMER

Culley, Margaret. "Elizabeth Meriwether (Dorothy Dix) Gilmer," in *Notable American Women, The Modern Period,* ed. by Barbara Sicherman and Carl Hurd Green. Cambridge, MA and London, England: The Belknap Press of Harvard University Press, 1980.

Dix, Dorothy. "Dictates for a Happy Life," from The Dorothy Dix Collection, F.G. Woodward Library, Austin Peay State University. Online, 1998. Available http://library.apsu.edu/dix/happy.htm. Accessed April 22, 1999.

Kane, Harnett T. with Ella Bentley Arthur. *Dear Dorothy Dix, the Story of A Compassionate Woman.* Garden City, NY: Doubleday & Company, 1952.

IDA B. WELLS BARNETT

Decosta-Willis, Miriam, ed. *The Memphis Diary of Ida B. Wells.* Boston: Beacon Press, 1995.

Duster, Alfreda M., ed. *Crusader for Justice, the Autobiography of Ida B. Wells.* Chicago: University of Chicago Press, 1970.

Hendricks, Wanda A. "Ida B. Wells-Barnett and the Alpha Suffrage Club of Chicago," in *One Woman, One Vote: Rediscovering the Woman Suffrage Movement,* ed. by Marjorie Spruill Wheeler. Troutdale, OR: NewSage Press, 1995.

Wynn, Linda T. "Ida B. Wells Barnett (1862–1930)," in *Profiles of African Americans in Tennessee,* ed. by Bobby L. Lovett and Linda T. Wynn. Nashville, TN: Annual Local Conference on Afro-American Culture and History, 1996.

———. "Ida B. Wells Barnett (1862–1930)," in *Notable Black American Women,* ed. by Jessie C. Smith. Detroit, MI: Gale Research, Inc., 1992.

Yellin, Carol Lynn and Janann Sherman, Ph.D. *The Perfect 36: Tennessee Delivers Woman Suffrage.* Memphis, TN: Vote 70 Inc., 1998.

EMMA BELL MILES

Galletta, Jan. "The Bird Watcher of Walden's Ridge," *Chattanooga News-Free Press,* January 8, 1984.

Gaston, Kay Baker. "Emma Bell Miles and the Fountain Square Conversations," *Tennessee Historical Quarterly.* Vol. 37, 1978.

BIBLIOGRAPHY

————. "Emma Bell Miles," *Signal Mountain Observer*, December 1975.

Latham, Sally. "Paintings of Emma Bell Miles to be Shown Sunday," *Chattanooga Times*, October 15, 1970.

Miles, Emma Bell. *The Spirit of the Mountains*. New York: J. Pott, 1905. Reprint. Knoxville, TN: University of Tennessee Press, 1975.

Rowell, Adelaide. "Emma Bell Miles, Artist, Author, and Poet of the Tennessee Mountains," *Tennessee Historical Quarterly*, Vol. 25, Spring 1966.

Veazy, Kathy. "The Story of Emma Bell Miles," *Chattanooga News-Free Press*, September 13, 1985.

EMMA ROCHELLE WHEELER

Livingood, James W. *Chattanooga and Hamilton County Medical Society: The Profession and Its Community*. Chattanooga, TN: Chattanooga and Hamilton County Medical Society, 1983.

Wynn, Linda T. "Emma Rochelle Wheeler (1882–1957)," in *Profiles of African Americans in Tennessee*, ed. by Bobby L. Lovett and Linda T. Wynn. Nashville, TN: Annual Local Conference on Afro-American Culture and History, 1996.

————. "Emma Rochelle Wheeler (1882–1957)," in *Notable Black American Women, Book II*, ed. by Jessie C. Smith. Detroit, MI: Gale Research, Inc., 1996.

SUE SHELTON WHITE

Huehls, Betty Sparks. "Sue Shelton White: The Making of a Radical," *West Tennessee Historical Society Papers*, Vol. 48, 1994.

Louis, James P. "Sue Shelton White and the Woman Suffrage Movement in Tennessee, 1913–1920," *Tennessee Historical Quarterly*, Vol. 22, 1963.

Wheeler, Marjorie Spruill, ed. *One Woman, One Vote: Rediscovering the Woman Suffrage Movement*. Troutdale, OR: NewSage Press, 1995.

————, ed. *Votes for Women!: The Woman Suffrage Movement in Tennessee, the South, and the Nation*. Knoxville, TN: University of Tennessee Press, 1995.

Yellin, Carol Lynn and Janann Sherman, Ph.D. *The Perfect 36: Tennessee Delivers Woman Suffrage*. Memphis, TN: Vote 70 Inc., 1998.

BESSIE SMITH

Bogle, Donald. *Brown Sugar*. New York: Harmony Books, 1980.

Friedwald, Will. *Jazz Singing*. New York: Charles Scribner's Sons, 1990.

Jones, Hettie. *Big Star Fallin' Mama, Five Women in Black Music*. New York: Viking Press, 1974.

Kay, Jackie. *Bessie Smith*. Somerset, England: Absolute Press, 1997.

Moore, Carmen. *Somebody's Angel Child, The Story of Bessie Smith*. New York: Thomas Y. Crowell Company, 1969.

Reitz, Rosetta. "Bessie Smith, 'Empress of the Blues': 1894–1937," in *Notable Black American Women*, ed. by Jessie C. Smith. Detroit, MI: Gale Research, Inc., 1992.

Smith, Whitney. "Legacy Still Hard-Driving 50 Years After Fatal Crash," *Memphis Commercial Appeal*, September 20, 1987.

Terkel, Studs. *Giants of Jazz*. New York: Thomas Y. Crowell Company, 1975.

GRACE MOORE

Farrar, Rowena Rutherford. *Grace Moore and Her Many Worlds*. New York: Cornwall Books, 1982.

Moore, Grace. *You're Only Human Once*. Garden City, NJ: Doubleday, Doran & Co., Inc., 1944.

INDEX

A

Accomac County, Virginia, 20
Adams, John Quincy, 25, 26
The Adventure (flatboat), 20
Alpha Kappa Alpha, 95
Alpha Suffrage Club, 80
American Literary, Scientific and Military
    Academy, 50
Andrew Johnson Historic Site, 46
Andrew Johnson Museum-Library, 46
Andrew Johnson National Cemetery, 46
Anthony, Susan B., 78
Armstrong, Louis, 113
Army of Tennessee, 24
Attakullakulla, 10, 12, 14

B

Bailey, Gwendolyn, 114
Barnett, Alfreda, 79
Barnett, Charles, 79
Barnett, Ferdinand L., 79
Barnett, Herman, 79
Barnett, Ida, 79
Barnett, Ida B. Wells, 6, 71–80
Barthelemy, Richard, 124
Bay Saint Louis, Mississippi, 63
Bean, Lydia, 13
Bean, William, 13
Beasley, James, 53
Bell, Benjamin Franklin, 83
Bell, Elmer, 83
Bell, Martha Ann Mirick, 83
Belle Meade Plantation, 47–51, 52, 53–54,
    57–58
Beloved Woman. *See* Ward, Nancy
Benton, Tennessee, 17
Berlin, Irving, 118, 123
Bessie Smith Revue, 115
Billboard, 116
Brown, John "Jack" Ellerson, 48

C

Calvary Baptist Church, 122
Canton, Georgia, 9
Carnton, 50, 51, 57
Carter County, Tennessee, 43
Catt, Carrie Chapman, 102, 103, 104
Century, 81, 86
Chase, Martha Gilmer, 62
Chattanooga, Tennessee, 93–96, 111
Chattanooga News, 87
Chattanooga Times, 94, 106
Cherokees, 8–16
Chesapeake, Ohio and Southwestern
    Railroad Company, 73
Chicago Civic Opera Company, 122
Chicago's Negro Fellowship League, 79
Childress, Anderson, 31
Childress, Benjamin, 31
Childress, Elizabeth, 31
Childress, Joel, 31
Childress, John, 31
Childress, Susan, 31
Chota, 10, 13, 16–17
Cincinnati Centennial Exposition, 37
civil rights, 71–80
Civil War, 37, 42–43, 47–50, 52–58
Clarksville, Tennessee, 62
Clay, Henry, 34
Cocke County, Tennessee, 121
Cohn, Harry, 125
Colbert, Claudette, 125
Columbia, Tennessee, 32
Columbian Exposition, 78
Columbia Pictures, 125
Columbia Recording Studio, 108, 110, 114, 115
Consumers Advisory Board, National
    Recovery Administration, 107
Cookman Institute, 93
County Atrium, Ireland, 50
Creeks, 8–9
Cumberland River, 20

D

Daily News, 126
Daily Picayune, 59, 63–64
Daughters of the American Revolution
   (DAR), Nancy Ward Chapter, 17
Democratic National Committee, 107
Diamond Jubilee, 64
Dickinson, Charles, 22
doctors. See Wheeler, Emma Rochelle
Donelson, Andrew Jackson, 23
Donelson, John, 20, 21
Donelson, Lizabeth, 23
Donelson, Samuel, 21, 23
Dorothy Dix. See Gilmer, Elizabeth
   Meriwether
Douglas, Frederick, 78
"Down-Hearted Blues," 110
Dragging Canoe, 14, 15
Dykeman, Wilma, 90

E

Early Jazz (Schuller), 117
Edison, Thomas, 108
Edison, Thomas A., 126
Emancipation Proclamation, 74
Equal Rights Amendment, 106
Evansville, Indiana, 83

F

Fall, George William, 37
Fall, Saidee Polk, 37
Far Away Meadows Farm, 127
Federal Security Agency, 107
Female Academy of Clarksville, 62
First Baptist Church (Chattanooga), 129
First Baptist Church (Jellico), 121
First Ladies. See Johnson, Eliza McCardle;
   Polk, Sarah Childress
Fisk University, 75
Fivekiller, 10
Forest Hills Cemetery, 129
Forrest, Nathan Bedford, 43
Fort Harrodsburg, 20
Fort Loudon, 11
Fort Mackinac, 52, 56
Fort Nashborough, 20
Fort Watauga, 13
Free Speech and Headlight, 76, 77

G

Gable, Clark, 125
Gainesville, Florida, 91
Garden, Mary, 122, 123, 124
Gee, Jack, 112
Georgetown Female Seminary, 42
Georgia Robertson Christian College, 101
Gilmer, Elizabeth Meriwether, 7, 59–70
Gilmer, George, 59, 62–63, 65, 66
Good Housekeeping, 65
Green, Juanita, 116
Greene County, Tennessee, 40
Greeneville, Tennessee, 40, 41, 46
Greeneville College, 40, 41
Gustav Adolph (prince of Sweden), 128
Gustav (king of Sweden), 127

H

Hampton, Lionel, 115
Harding, Elizabeth McGavock, 47–58
Harding, John, 50, 51, 53
Harding, Mary Elizabeth, 51–52
Harding, Nathaniel, 51
Harding, Sarah Susan, 51
Harding, Selene, 51
Harding, William Giles, 47, 50–53, 54–55,
   56–58
Harper's, 83
Hayes, Lucy, 37
Hayes, Rutherford B., 37
Hearst, William Randolph, 64
Henderson, Fletcher, 113
Henderson, Tennessee, 100
Hermitage, 23, 24, 26, 27
Highland Cemetery, 96
Hitchy Koo (musical), 123
Hiwassee Purchase, 16
Holliday, Billie, 115, 117
Hollins Institute, 62
Holly Springs, Mississippi, 74
Hopewell, Treaty of, 15
Horseshoe Bend, Battle of, 23
House of Representatives, 24, 25, 38. See also
   U.S. House of Representatives
Houston, Sam, 50
Howard, Joseph, Jr., 93
Howard, Joseph R., 93
Hubbard Hospital, 96

Huff, John A., 129
Hunter, Alberta, 117
Hunter's Hill Plantation, 23

I

Ida B. Wells Women's Club, 79
Indianapolis World, 76
Iola. *See* Barnett, Ida B. Wells
It Happened One Night (film), 125

J

Jackson, Andrew, 6, 18–20, 21, 22–27, 29, 32, 33, 34, 50
Jackson, Andrew, Jr., 23
Jackson, Mahalia, 117
Jackson, Rachel Donelson, 6, 18–28
Jackson, Tennessee, 101
Jackson Business & Professional Women's Club, 107
Jellico, Tennessee, 121
Jetton, Sarah Polk "Sallie," 37
Johnson, Andrew, 38–46, 52, 54, 55, 57
Johnson, Andrew, Jr. "Frank," 42, 43, 45
Johnson, Charles, 42, 43
Johnson, Eliza McCardle, 38–46
Johnson, Martha (later Martha Patterson), 41, 42
Johnson, Robert, 42, 45
Joplin, Janis, 116
journalists. *See* Barnett, Ida B. Wells; Gilmer, Elizabeth Meriwether

K

Kahn, Otto, 118, 124
Kern, Jerome, 123
Kingfisher, 8–9
King's Mountain, Battle of, 14

L

La Bohème (Puccini), 120
A Lady's Morals (film), 125
Ledger Syndicate, 67
Lincoln, Abraham, 41, 42, 44
Lincoln, Mordecai, 41
Lippincott's, 83
Living Way, 76
Louise (film), 127

Love, Earl, 112
lynching, 76–79

M

Martinelli, Giovanni, 122
Mary (queen of England), 127
Maury County, Tennessee, 32
McCardle, John, 40
McGavock, Elizabeth Irwin (later Elizabeth Harding), 50
McGavock, Randal, 50
McGavock, Sarah Rodgers, 50, 56
McKellar, Kenneth, 106
McNairy, Selena, 51
McSpadden's Bend Plantation, 51
Meharry Medical, Dental, and Pharmaceutical College, 93
Memphis, Tennessee, 74–77
Meriwether, Edward, 62
Meriwether, Mary, 62
Meriwether, William Douglas, 62, 63
Metro-Goldwyn-Mayer Studios (MGM), 125
Metropolitan Opera, 118, 120, 123–24
Middletown, Connecticut, 50
Miles, Emma Bell, 6, 81–90
Miles, G. Frank, 83–84
Miles, Jean, 86
Miles, Joe, 86
Miles, Judith, 86
Miles, Kittie, 86
Miles, Mark, 86
Montezuma, Tennessee, 100
Montgomery County, Tennessee, 61
Moore, Grace, 118–29
Moore, Mary Willie Grace. *See* Moore, Grace
Moore, Richard, 121, 122, 123
Moore, Tessie, 120
Moravian Academy, 31
Morgan, Richard, 115
Moses Stokes Traveling Show, 112
Mount Lawn Cemetery, 116
Murfreesboro, Tennessee, 31
Music Box Revue (Berlin), 118, 123

N

NAACP, 79, 96, 116
Nancy Ward Chapter, Daughters of the American Revolution (DAR), 17

Nanye'hi. *See* Ward, Nancy
Nashville, Battle of, 57
Nashville, Tennessee, 21, 22, 27, 50, 93, 96
Nashville American, 63
Nashville Union, 36
Natchez, Mississippi, 21
The Nation, 105
Nation, Carrie, 64
National American Woman's Suffrage
    Association (NAWSA), 80, 102
National Association for the Advancement of
    Colored People (NAACP), 79, 96, 116
National Service Fellowship Medal, 126
National Theater, 122
National Women's Party (NWP), 97–99,
    102, 103
Native Americans, 8–17
NAWSA, 80, 102, 104
New Moon (film), 125
New Orleans, Battle of, 24
New Orleans, Louisiana, 63, 66, 67
New York Age, 76, 77
New York Journal, 64–65
New York Times, 123
Nicholson, Eliza, 63
Nineteenth Amendment, 99, 106
"Nobody Knows You When You're Down
    and Out," 115
Nurse Service Club of Chattanooga, 95
Nuttall, Thomas, 10
NWP, 97–99, 102, 103, 104, 105

O

Oglethorpe University, 66
Okeh Records, 115
Old Hickory. *See* Jackson, Andrew
Old Hop, 10
One Night of Love (film), 125, 126
One Night of Love (song), 126
Osconostato, 10
Our Southern Birds (Miles), 90

P

Parera, Valentin, 125
Parks, Rosa, 73
Patterson, David T., 42, 44
Patterson, Martha Johnson, 44, 45, 46
Pete Werley's Florida Cotton Blossoms, 112
Phillips, Sarah, 40
Pittsylvania County, Virginia, 20

Polk, James Knox, 29, 31–35, 36–37, 50
Polk, Samuel, 32
Polk, Sarah Childress, 29–37, 52
Polk Place, 36–37
Pott, James, and Company, 84
presidential campaigns, 25–27
Putnam's, 83

Q

Queen Victoria's Diamond Jubilee, 64
Quincy, Illinois, 62

R

Rabbit Foot Minstrels, 112
Rabbit Hash, Kentucky, 83
Radio City Music Hall, 125
Raffe, Rowena, 123
Rainey, Gertrude "Ma," 112
*A Red Record: Tabulated Statistics and Alleged Causes
    of Lynching in the United States* (Barnett), 79
Reitz, Rosetta, 110
Rhea Academy, 40
Ricketson, Anna, 81
Robards, Lewis, 18, 20–22
Roberts, Albert H., 105
Robertson, James, 11
Rochelle, Ella, 93
Rochelle, William, 93
Royal Proclamation of 1763, 11–12
Rucker, Johanna, 35
Rutherford County, Tennessee, 31
Rutledge, Tennessee, 41

S

Salem, North Carolina, 31
Saunders, Gertrude, 115
Schertzinger, Victor, 126
Schuller, Gunther, 117
Sevier, John, 14–15
Shaw University, 74
Shelby County, Tennessee, 71
Signal Mountain, 83
Simpson, Wallis Warfield, 127
Sixteenth Brigade, Tennessee Militia, 50
Slabtown, Tennessee, 121
Smith, Andrew, 111
Smith, Bessie, 6, 108–17
Smith, Clarence, 108, 110, 112
Smith, Hugh, 116
Smith, Laura, 111

Smith, William, 111
Social Security Board, 107
Society of Arts and Sciences, 126
Sousa, John Philip, 126
Southall, Mary McGavock, 56
The Spirit of the Mountains (Miles), 84–86, 90
St. Louis Blues, 114
State Department's Cultural Exchange
    Program, 128
Stockley, Rachel, 20
Stover, Daniel, 42, 43
Stover, Mary Johnson, 43, 44
suffrage movement. *See* Barnett, Ida B. Wells;
    White, Sue Shelton
Suffragist, 105
Suite Sixteen (musical), 123
Sumner County, Tennessee, 31

T

Taliwa, Battle of, 8–9
Tame Deer, 10
Tame Doe, 10
Tennessee Equal Suffrage Association
    (TESA), 102, 103
Tennessee Militia, 14
Tennessee Supreme Court, 24, 73, 75–76,
    101
Trail of Tears, 16
Treaty of Hopewell, 15
Tulane University, 66
Tusculum College, 46
Tyler, John, 34
Tyler, Julia, 34

U

U.S. House of Representatives, 32–33. *See also*
    House of Representatives
U.S. Secretary of War, 24
U.S. Senate, 24, 25, 38, 42, 45–46
USO, 128

V

Van Buren, John, 36
Vevay, Indiana, 43
Virginia House of Burgesses, 20

W

Walden Hospital, 94–96
Walden's Ridge, Tennessee, 81, 83, 86–87,
    88, 89, 90
Walden's Ridge Historical Society, 90
Walden University, 93
Walker, Frank, 108, 110, 113, 114
Walker, James Knox, 35
Ward, Bryant, 11
Ward, Elisabeth, 11
Ward, Nancy, 8–17
Ward-Belmont School for Girls, 121
Warrensburg, Tennessee, 41
Warrenton, Elizabeth, 74
Washington College of Law, 106
Wells, James, 74
Werner, Kate, 103
West Tennessee Business College, 101
Wheeler, Betty, 95
Wheeler, Emma Rochelle, 91–96
Wheeler, George, 95
Wheeler, John N., 93
Wheeler, Thelma, 95
Wheeler Newspaper Syndicate, 66
Whig Party, 34
White, James Shelton, 100
White, Mary Calistia Swain, 100
White, Sue Shelton, 6, 97–107
Whitsett, Elizabeth, 31
Wiley Memorial Methodist Church, 96
Wilson, Woodrow, 97, 99
Wilson-Greene School of Music, 122
Windsor, Duke of, 127
Winston, Maria, 62
Woodstock, 62, 71
World War I, 65
World War II, 67, 68, 127–28

Y

Younger, Maude, 102
Young Men's Christian Association (YMCA),
    79

About the Author

Susan Sawyer enjoys exploring the past and writing about historical topics. History serves as the centerpiece for many of her writings, taking the form of both fact and fiction. Drawing upon her fascination with the history of her native South, Susan has written seven historical and contemporary romance novels. She is also the author of several books about the historical growth and development of individual companies and organizations. *More than Petticoats: Remarkable Tennessee Women* is Susan's twelfth book.

A graduate of the University of Tennessee, Susan worked as a magazine editor and communications consultant before establishing a career as a freelance writer and published author. Today, she writes full-time from her home in Tennessee, where she lives with her husband, Ron, and their miniature schnauzer, Maxwell Smart Sawyer.

More than Petticoats series

With in-depth and accurate coverage, this series pays tribute to the often unheralded efforts and achievements of the women who settled the West. Each title in the series includes a collection of absorbing biographies and b&w historical photos.

TWODOT
An Imprint of Falcon Publishing

More than Petticoats:
Remarkable North Carolina Women
by Scotti Kent
$12.95
ISBN 1-56044-900-4

More than Petticoats:
Remarkable California Women
by Erin H. Turner
$9.95
ISBN 1-56044-859-8

More than Petticoats:
Remarkable Montana Women
by Gayle C. Shirley
$8.95
ISBN 1-56044-363-4

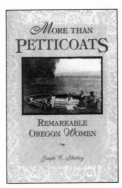

More than Petticoats:
Remarkable Oregon Women
by Gayle C. Shirley
$9.95
ISBN 1-56044-668-4

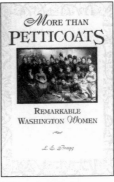

More than Petticoats:
Remarkable Washington Women
by L.E. Bragg
$9.95
ISBN 1-56044-667-6

TwoDot™ features books that celebrate and interpret the rich culture and history of regional America.

It Happened in *Series from TwoDot™ Books*

An imprint of Falcon Publishing

TWODOT™

Featured in this series are fascinating stories about events that helped shape each state's history. Written in a lively, easy-to-read style, each book features 31-34 stories for history buffs of all ages. Entertaining and informative, each book is 6x9" and features b&w illustrations.

It Happened in Arizona
It Happened in Colorado
It Happened in Georgia
It Happened in Massachusetts
It Happened in Montana
It Happened in New Mexico
It Happened in New York
It Happened in North Carolina
It Happened in Northern California
It Happened in Oregon
It Happened in Southern California
It Happened in Texas
It Happened in Utah
It Happened in Washington

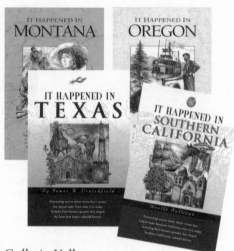

More from TwoDot™ Books

Bozeman and the Gallatin Valley
Charlie's Trail: The Life and Art of C.M. Russell
Flight of the Dove: The Story of Jeannette Rankin
Growing up Western
Heart of the Trail: The Stories of Eight Wagon Train Women
Jeannette Rankin: Bright Star in the Big Sky
Men with Sand: Great Explorers of the American West
Montana Campfire Tales: Fourteen Historical Essays
More Than Petticoats: Remarkable Montana Women
More Than Petticoats: Remarkable Oregon Women
More Than Petticoats: Remarkable Tennessee Women
More Than Petticoats: Remarkable Washington Women
The Champion Buffalo Hunter
The Only Good Bear is a Dead Bear
Today I Baled Some Hay to Feed the Sheep the Coyotes Eat

The TwoDot line features classic western literature and history. Each book celebrates and interprets the vast spaces and rich culture of the American West.

FALCON®

To order check with your local bookseller or call Falcon® at

1-800-582-2665

Ask for a FREE catalog featuring a complete list of titles on nature, outdoor recreation, travel and regional history.

www.falcon.com

FALCON GUIDES® Leading the way™

FalconGuides® are available for where-to-go hiking, mountain biking, rock climbing, walking, scenic driving, fishing, rockhounding, paddling, birding, wildlife viewing, and camping. We also have FalconGuides on essential outdoor skills and subjects and field identification. The following titles are currently available, but this list grows every year. For a free catalog with a complete list of titles, call FALCON toll-free at 1-800-582-2665.

BIRDING GUIDES

Birding Georgia
Birding Illinois
Birding Minnesota
Birding Montana
Birding Northern California
Birding Texas
Birding Utah

PADDLING GUIDES

Paddling Minnesota
Paddling Montana
Paddling Okefenokee
Paddling Oregon
Paddling Yellowstone & Grand
   Teton National Parks

WALKING

Walking Colorado Springs
Walking Denver
Walking Portland
Walking Seattle
Walking St. Louis
Walking San Francisco
Walking Virginia Beach

CAMPING GUIDES

Camping Arizona
Camping California's
   National Forests
Camping Colorado
Camping Oregon
Camping Southern California
Camping Washington
Recreation Guide to Washington
   National Forests

FIELD GUIDES

Bitterroot: Montana State Flower
Canyon Country Wildflowers
Central Rocky Mountain
   Wildflowers
Chihuahuan Desert Wildflowers
Great Lakes Berry Book
New England Berry Book
Ozark Wildflowers
Pacific Northwest Berry Book
Plants of Arizona
Rare Plants of Colorado
Rocky Mountain Berry Book
Scats & Tracks of the Pacific
   Coast States
Scats & Tracks of the Rocky Mtns.
Sierra Nevada Wildflowers
Southern Rocky Mountain
   Wildflowers
Tallgrass Prairie Wildflowers
Western Trees

ROCKHOUNDING GUIDES

Rockhounding Arizona
Rockhounding California
Rockhounding Colorado
Rockhounding Montana
Rockhounding Nevada
Rockhounding New Mexico
Rockhounding Texas
Rockhounding Utah
Rockhounding Wyoming

HOW-TO GUIDES

Avalanche Aware
Backpacking Tips
Bear Aware
Desert Hiking Tips
Hiking with Dogs
Hiking with Kids
Mountain Lion Alert
Reading Weather
Route Finding
Using GPS
Wild Country Companion
Wilderness First Aid
Wilderness Survival

MORE GUIDEBOOKS

Backcountry Horseman's
   Guide to Washington
Family Fun in Montana
Family Fun in Yellowstone
Exploring Canyonlands & Arches
   National Parks
Exploring Hawaii's Parklands
Exploring Mount Helena
Exploring Southern California
   Beaches
Hiking Hot Springs of the Pacific
   Northwest
Touring Arizona Hot Springs
Touring California & Nevada
   Hot Springs
Touring Colorado Hot Springs
Touring Montana and Wyoming
   Hot Springs
Trail Riding Western Montana
Wilderness Directory
Wild Montana
Wild Utah
Wild Virginia

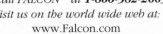

■ *To order any of these books, check with your local bookseller or call FALCON ® at 1-800-582-2665.*
Visit us on the world wide web at:
www.Falcon.com

FALCON®

FALCONGUIDES ® Leading the Way™

www.Falcon.com

Since 1979, Falcon® has brought you the best in outdoor recreational guidebooks.
Now you can access that same reliable and accurate information online.

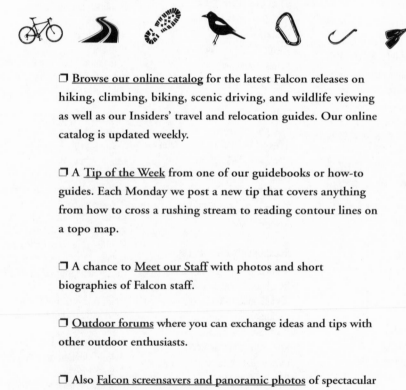

❏ <u>Browse our online catalog</u> for the latest Falcon releases on
hiking, climbing, biking, scenic driving, and wildlife viewing
as well as our Insiders' travel and relocation guides. Our online
catalog is updated weekly.

❏ A <u>Tip of the Week</u> from one of our guidebooks or how-to
guides. Each Monday we post a new tip that covers anything
from how to cross a rushing stream to reading contour lines on
a topo map.

❏ A chance to <u>Meet our Staff</u> with photos and short
biographies of Falcon staff.

❏ <u>Outdoor forums</u> where you can exchange ideas and tips with
other outdoor enthusiasts.

❏ Also <u>Falcon screensavers and panoramic photos</u> of spectacular
destinations.

And much more!

Plan your next outdoor adventure at our web site. Point your browser to
www.Falcon.com and get FalconGuided!

FALCON®